Hunting and Gathering in the Corporate Tribe

Hunting and Gathering in the Corporate Tribe

Archetypes of the Corporate Culture

Keith Wilcock

Algora Publishing
New York

© 2004 by Algora Publishing.
All Rights Reserved
www.algora.com

No portion of this book (beyond what is permitted by
Sections 107 or 108 of the United States Copyright Act of 1976)
may be reproduced by any process, stored in a retrieval system,
or transmitted in any form, or by any means, without the
express written permission of the publisher.
ISBN: 0-87586-250-0 (softcover)
ISBN: 0-87586-251-9 (hardcover)
ISBN: 0-87586-198-9 (ebook)

Library of Congress Cataloging-in-Publication Data

Wilcock, Keith D.
  Hunting and gathering in the corporate tribe / by Keith D. Wilcock.
    p. ; cm.
  Includes index.
    ISBN 0-87586-250-0 (trade paper) — ISBN 0-87586-251-9 (hard cover) — ISBN 0-87586-198-9 (e-book)
  1. Corporate culture. 2. Business anthropology. 3. Psychology, Industrial. I. Title.

HD58.7.W527 2003
302.3'5—dc22
                           2003027408

Printed in the United States

The theory that corporations are evolved tribes opens entirely new ways of thinking about and analyzing modern business organizations. *Hunting and Gathering in the Corporate Tribe* shows how to apply the new field of *corporate anthropology* to the every day challenges of operating a business. Watch out. This book will shift your paradigm.

Dr. Marvin Dunnette, Fellow and Past President
of The Society of Industrial and Organizational Psychologists

Table of Contents

Introduction	1
PART ONE	
Corporate Archetypes	7
Chapter One	
Archetypes in Corporations	9
Anima and Animus	10
Multiple Tribal Affiliations	12
Chapter Two	
Soft- vs. Hard-Style Management	17
Anima as Bread Winner	18
Tribal Day Care	20
Chapter Three	
Gathering in Corporate Tribes	23
Gathering as Shopping	25
Nurturing in Corporations	27
Anima and Corporate Profits	30
What Makes a Good Corporate Gatherer	31
How to Reward Corporate Gatherers	33
The Velvet Carpet	35
Vulnerabilities and Blind Spots	36
Chapter Four	
On the Evolution of Animus	39
Warriors, Infanticide, and Cannibalism	40
The New Warriors	41
The Warrior Fire and Teenage Crime	42
The Recent Emergence of the Father Role	45

CHAPTER FIVE
CORPORATE HUNTING 47
   Weapons 47
   Buffalo Robes 49
   Corporate Hunters 50
   How to Develop Corporate Hunters 51
   The Corporate War Dance 52
   Marketing as Scouting 52

CHAPTER SIX
CORPORATE WARFARE 55
   Territory 57
   Missiles and Bombs 62
   Paintball Battles 62

CHAPTER SEVEN
THE WIZARD ARCHETYPE 67
   Wizards in Mythology and Real Life 70
   Dens of Wizards 70
   Corporate Wizards 71
   Burning the Bitches 72
   Use of Archetypes in Career Counseling 74
   The Evolution of Tribal Wizards 76

CHAPTER EIGHT
THE CHIEF ARCHETYPE 77
   God Kings 79
   Identifying Alpha 80
   Compensation and the Dominance Hierarchy .. 83
   Alpha and Sexual Appetite 84
   Alpha and Vision 85
   The Alpha Role 87

CHAPTER NINE
THE COUNCIL OF ELDERS 91

CHAPTER TEN
THE TROOPS 95

CHAPTER ELEVEN
ON BECOMING A CORPORATE TRIBE 101
   The Actualized Corporate Tribe 103

PART TWO
WORLD CULTURES VS. THE CORPORATE CULTURE — 105

CHAPTER TWELVE
THE WORLD'S VARIOUS CULTURES — 107
- Corporate Culture — 108
- The Real Corporate Culture — 109
- Tribes — 111

CHAPTER THIRTEEN
THE RELENTLESS SPREAD OF THE CORPORATE CULTURE — 115
- Business School Wizards — 117
- Accounting Rules as Corporate Mores — 118
- Globalization — 121
- The New Corporate Loyalty — 124
- Job Hoppers and Downsizers — 129
- Corporate Greed — 130
- Corporate Democracy — 132
- The Tribeless Remainder — 133
- Where is Grandpa? — 136

PART THREE
NATION-STATES AND MULTINATIONAL CORPORATIONS AS WORLD TRIBES — 139

CHAPTER FOURTEEN
NATION-STATES AS TRIBES — 141
- The USA as a Tribe — 142
- Political Dynasties — 146
- Corporations and the Evolution of Nation-States — 147
- Economic Sanctions — 149
- Multinational Teams — 152
- Corporations and Nation-State Identity — 153

CHAPTER FIFTEEN
THE CORPORATE CULTURE IN CHINA — 157
- The Rising Sun — 161
- The Pacific Impulse — 162
- The Corporate Culture in the Middle East — 164

PART FOUR
CORPORATE CULTURE VS. THE AGRICULTURAL INSTITUTIONS OF ORGANIZED RELIGION AND WAR — 169

Chapter Sixteen
The Evolution of Religious Belief   171
    Evil and the War on Drugs   173
    Myths that Murder   175
    Castles, Cathedrals, and Skyscrapers   177
    Corporations and the Religion of Science   178
    Intelligence Testing and Succession   180
    When Culture Clash   184
    The Devastating Impact of Corporate Culture   185
    Religious Fundamentalists vs. the Corporate Culture   186

Chapter Seventeen
Corporations and the Evolution of War   191
    Does the Eagle Hunt for Flies?   196
    Defusing Jihad   198

Chapter Eighteen
Spreading the Corporate Culture   203
    Closing Remarks   204

Index   209

Introduction

When a corporation fires all the top executives of a recently acquired company, it is following an ancient tribal formula. Putting all the adult men to the sword was standard practice when one tribe conquered another. Yet those executives who wield the axe are completely unaware of the true roots of their behavior. When asked, they invariably have a logical business explanation for their decision.

Very few members of the board of directors realize that the role they fulfill, the council of elders, exists in all human clusters, on all continents, in all cultures. Even the room they meet in, the wood-paneled boardroom with its huge table and portraits of past presidents, evolved down through the ages from the men's huts and council chambers of primitive tribes.

Corporations still employ hunters and gatherers but neither the people who hire them or the employees themselves are aware that they are fulfilling ancient tribal roles.

Seeing one's corporation as a tribe and understanding one's archetypal role within it, an employee can begin to discern the underlying meanings of coded messages, and the motives that drive executives. At the same time, executives and employees alike gain a new understanding of the tools used to increase motivation, elicit loyalty, and induce people to become committed to company goals.

Corporations are evolved tribes. They are like hybrids or mutations. The corporation is a human cluster whose goal is to survive and grow; it provides for its people, and competes with and defends against other tribes. The direct violence of earlier tribal life has, in many ways, been softened.

Corporations still *fire* people, but they don't actually burn them up. People get terminated but not really killed. Thousands of top-level executives get the ax, but not the executioner's ax; most get back up, dust themselves off and head out in search of a safe haven with another corporation.

Feelings are hurt, great fortunes are made and lost. The politics are often ruthless, frustrating and complex. The pressure and stress can cause illness. But there are no physical beatings, and there is no need to worry that the corporation across the hall or down the street will be throwing spears at you or conducting armed raids on your office.

In the first one or two hundred years of their emergence, these new tribal mutations we know as corporations have acquired a tremendous power and influence. The changes they are driving are every bit as profound, possibly more profound, than the changes brought about ten thousand years ago when humankind discovered agriculture.

Thanks to the research efforts of archeologists, our knowledge of upper Paleolithic (20,000 B.C.), Mesolithic (10,000 B.C.), and Neolithic (4,000 B.C.) societies as well as Bronze Age and Iron Age people is expanding dramatically. Careful analysis of artifacts and bone fragments are providing factual evidence of both the direction and rate of migrations as well as the spread of knowledge of new and better food-getting techniques and methods. Among the several great books that detail results of this research are *Guns, Germs, and Steel* by Jared Diamond[1], and *Women's Work, the First 20,000 Years* by Elizabeth Wayland Barber.[2]

Learning to grow their own food changed every aspect of people's daily life. The first permanent settlements emerged. The first nation-states, the first storage of food and accumulations of wealth, the first armies, the first organized religions, the relentless transformation of hunting grounds into cultivated crop producing fields; all this evolved from the discovery of new methods of obtaining food.

This process of transformation is still being played out in the last surviving pockets of hunting and gathering societies, for example in the jungles of Brazil. The surface of the earth began to change from hunting grounds to cultivated farmland ten thousand years ago and this process is still going on.

---

1. Diamond, Jared, *Guns, Germs, and Steel, The Fates of Human Societies* (New York: W. W. Norton & Company, 1999).

2. Barber, Elizabeth Wayland, *Women's Work, The First 20,000 Years* (New York: W. W. Norton & Company, 1994).

However, two or three generations ago, another change began to take root. Corporations emerged and began to grow, and massive new migrations began. Like the giant "magnets" that suck wildebeest and caribou on their annual migrations, millions of farmers began to move to the cities, to the factories and offices of the new tribal mutations. Unlike the caribou and wildebeest, most of them never went back. In Europe and the United States, 90% of our grandfathers were farmers. That number has almost reversed, so that 90% of us now work in cities, small businesses and corporations. In industrialized countries, the population of farmers has shrunk to below 10%.

Bees die to preserve and protect their hives. Perhaps it is the hive, an inanimate thing manufactured by insects, that is the primary survival unit, not the individual bee. What about us?

We experience life as individuals. We struggle against the elements, germs, diseases and human enemies to survive and live. Perhaps it is natural for us to focus so much of our attention on the study of the individual human. We hunger to understand the workings of the human mind and constantly focus attention on our own bodies and organs as we combat diseases and injuries.

But like bees, Homo sapiens are gregarious, colonizing creatures.

When Freud attempted to explain our basic survival drive as the primary motivator of human behavior, something did not seem to fit. During World War I, there were many reports of soldiers who fell on hand grenades in order to save their comrades. This behavior certainly did not reflect an individual drive for survival.

Perhaps it is the cluster, the hive, the tribe that is the most fundamental survival unit for humans. Even the notion of "survival of the fittest" clearly applies to corporations.

Being trapped within our own individual life experiences creates a certain blindness about tribes. Every bee has is role in helping its hive survive. Some are called upon to attack enemies and die. We humans do the same, as thousands of our fathers and grandfathers who died in various battles demonstrate. They fight and die for their tribes. Dying for one's country is seen as heroic in all human cultures.

Each species of animal has its own type of cluster. Elephants survive best in herds. Lions do so in prides. Fish form schools and birds form flocks. An animal's particular cluster may be an essential piece of its survival formula. Humans survive in tribes. Bee is to hive as human is to tribe.

In fact, corporations may be more like hives than were the tribes of agriculturalists. Farming requires close contact with the land, so people were more spread out. Their tribes were, to some extent, churches, and for some the armies and governing bodies of nation-states. Now 90% of these farmers are commuting into the big city, swarming down freeways to meet with their tribes, five days each week. Cities, as we know them, are relatively new in the evolution of mankind. From a distance, they look like gigantic clusters of ant-hills. Each corporation consists of hundreds of cells, almost like honeycombs, and several corporations are often literally stacked on top of one another in buildings that are every bit like the stacked boxes that bee farmers provide to their hives.

It is certain that humans feel a natural inclination, a drive, to form clusters. As the species evolves, we now realize that the shape and nature of human clusters, too, is evolving. Yet, even with all these profound changes, many of the same values, beliefs, ceremonies, relationships, and life roles that existed in the first human tribes can be easily detected just beneath the surface of the corporation. These most basic and fundamental roles, our human archetypes, are evolving as the worldwide corporate culture takes root. The process is still in its early stages.

It is imperative that we understand these newest kinds of human clusters. Because so many of us spend so much of our lives in corporations, we need to understand how they affect us, how they shape our beliefs, priorities and world views, and how they dictate our relationships to others and to the rest of the world. Understanding basic tribal dynamics gives us a better chance of satisfying our own needs and aspirations within a corporate career.

How do corporations differ from earlier tribal adaptations, and in what ways do they remain locked in that ancient tribal groove? The inner workings of corporations including such giants as General Motors, City Bank, Con Agra, Pepsi, Philips, Carlson Companies, Northwest Airlines reveal that each one mimics the patterns of tribal behavior. Local difference, "customs," are relatively minor; their similarities are greater than their differences.

Research into primitive tribes offers a valuable perspective that can increase our understanding of these organizations, as well as every individual's role in them and relation to them, and how they relate to each other.

Introduction

Helping employees and executives to recognize the tribal nature of their companies and to understand the tribal roles they are performing will enhance the corporation's ability to compete, survive and grow. Understanding tribal roles can be a key skill in career counseling; it can help corporate managers find their most appropriate tribal role, their best and most satisfying career path. This is true for every function in the corporation: for those who are, in fact, tribal chiefs, and for those who make up the tribe.

An understanding of tribal warfare can help corporations analyze their competitors, evaluate their weapons and growth strategies, understand their current territories, and formulate their marketing and sales campaigns. Training sessions using paint ball battles can be used to bring out the warrior aggressiveness of the field sales force, and week-long adventure team-building programs can promote bonding and build allegiance within management teams.

If the hunters hunt well and the gatherers gather well; if the financial and engineering wizards do their magic, and the field generals and troops continue to hold their territories and expand into new ones; and if the chief and sub chiefs provide effective leadership, their tribes will grow and prosper.

The basic theory that corporations are evolved tribes is presented in *The Corporate Tribe*. It traces changes in the basic tribal roles as human civilization progressed from hunting and gathering to agriculture, and then again when corporations burst forth, about 100 years ago. Applying concepts of Corporate Anthropology to large corporations proves that the model is apt. Recognizing that modern corporations are tribal mutations sheds light on the true meaning of corporate culture and how the spread of corporate methods and values is changing politics, religions, and war.

PART ONE

CORPORATE ARCHETYPES

CHAPTER ONE:
ARCHETYPES IN CORPORATIONS

The phrase "Corporate Archetypes" sounds like an oxymoron. How can something like a corporation, so recent in the evolution of human kind, be blended with something so ancient as an archetype? Still, if archetypes really are locked permanently into our brain stems, if they really do represent strands of the collective unconscious, if they really are numinous as Jung and others have proposed — then they must find expression now, in our times, even in our steel and glass skyscrapers, our metal honeycomb people hives, the ones we swarm to each weekday morning like bees.

Our ancient archetypes *do* find expression in modern corporations. Anima and Animus, cloaked in the pin-stripped regalia of the corporate tribe, still throb just beneath the surface. These archetypes influence the height of the glass ceiling, the bonding of men and women within corporations, patterns of coaching and mentoring, the quality of customer service, marketing and sales strategies, the effectiveness of leadership, even the approach a corporation takes to acquisitions and mergers.

The hunting and gathering methods that humans have used to promote the survival and growth of their earliest clusters, tribes, are still essential for survival in modern corporations; but these activities have evolved. We now know *hunting an gathering* as *sales and service.*

The wizards and court priests of earlier times are now scientists, financial gurus, computer whizzes, high-powered attorneys, design engineers, and industrial psychologists.

The chiefs and sub chiefs are the easiest to recognize. They have become CEOs and Division Vice Presidents.

The council of elders is now the Board of Directors.

The slaves, serfs, peons and untouchables of the agricultural era have evolved into hourly, non-exempt, blue collar workers.

These tribal roles are archetypal because they have been a part of every person's life experience since the beginning of time. Like the sun, the moon, and the stars, they have always been there.

ANIMA AND ANIMUS

The evolving roles of women and men in corporations may be the single most dramatic change in this latest mutation of human clusters. We are evolving away from gender-specific roles.

To understand this profound evolutionary trend, one needs to read the work of female anthropologists such as Martin and Voorhies. In their book *Female of the Species*[3], the bias resulting from the predominant male viewpoint in anthropology is clearly described. For example, descriptions of early Homo sapiens as "pack-hunting carnivores" refers only to men. In the same way, many tribal histories from the Bible to *The Rise and Fall of the Third Reich* focus only on chiefs, kings, or great male leaders, and their battles and struggles for territorial dominance. One almost needs to be reminded that these histories ignore half of the world's population.

In earlier tribes, *all* the hunters were men, and *all* the gatherers were women. Modern corporate tribes have many female hunters, and many male gatherers. Corporate sales representatives endure heavy travel, perform under the pressure of difficult sales goals and objectives, take the lead role in building and maintaining a customer base, and carry major responsibility for feeding the tribe. Although many corporations have struggled with the idea of female sales representatives (which used to be sales*men*), they now know that there are women who can do this job (and probably any other) as well as men.

Carl Jung did more writing on archetypes than anyone before, and it is ironic that he, the great interpreter of Animus, held some blind prejudices

---

3. Martin, Kay M. and Voorhies, Barbara, *Female of the Species* (New York: Columbia University Press, 1975).

against women. His book, *Aspects of the Feminine*, contains assertions that some readers would find outright offensive in today's America. For example, Jung wrote, "In intellectual women the Animus encourages a critical disputatiousness and would-be highbrowism, which, however, consists essentially in harping on some irrelevant weak point and nonsensically making it the main one.[4] Some would take the different mind-set in a different light and look at it as a quality. In general, women have a higher propensity to give attention to detailed work over a sustained period of time.

But if men often miss the mark in writing about women, the reverse is also likely. The ruthless streak that may be an essential element in defending one's territory, protecting one's family, killing animals for food, and in the less bloody scrambling for position in the corporate pecking order, has never been understood fully by large numbers of women.

The millions of man-hours spent watching football, basketball, hockey, and soccer on TV and in various sports arenas suggest that some deep internal need that is clearly stronger in men is being satisfied. These evolved tribal warfare rituals appear to satisfy some innate hunger that is more powerful and compelling in men than in women. Of course, there are huge overlaps — there are women who enjoy boxing and ball games, and men who enjoy shopping and dislike football, hunting, and competing for dominance.

Still, there appears to be a polarity between the Anima and Animus archetypes. At one pole is the nurturance of Anima. Its opposite is the ruthlessness of Animus. If giving life, growing, and nurturing is one pole, its opposite pole is taking life, destroying, dominating and controlling.

These forces exist in both men and women. Deep within each woman lurks a she-bear. All that is required to call forth her fierceness is an open threat to her children. Conversely, after Mike Tyson destroyed Frank Bruno in the third round with a series of truly vicious left hooks and uppercuts, he went to Bruno's corner, kissed his opponent's bowed head and patted him gently on the shoulder.

Each of us has a mother within us. Each of us has a warrior within us. How can these powerful gut level forces, polished by thousands of years of evolution,

---

4. Jung, C. G., *Aspects of the Feminine* (Princeton, New Jersey: Princeton University Press, 1982).

be understood, harnessed, controlled and applied to drive the growth and survival of modern corporations?

Anima is a highly complex blend of images. Jung lists among the images of "mother" one's personal mother, grandmother, stepmother, and mother-in-law, as well as such mother surrogates as governess and nurse. Add to this such spiritual images as the Mother of God, the Virgin, and a large cast of goddesses such as Ishtar, Isis, Diana, Kali, Shiva, Artemis and Sophia.

Anima symbols go far beyond the "mother" category. Blended into this rich archetype are symbols of daughters, baby girls, maidens, temptresses, queens, princesses, harlots, witches, and crones.

The Animus archetype is equally rich and complex in all its intricate expressions of the male gender. There is the father image, the grandfather, God, the king, the son, grandson, the bouncing baby boy, the wizard, priest, shaman, and brujo, the hunter and warrior, the rapist, hit man, law man and warden. The chief, president, pope, czar and headman must be included as well as prophet, jester, prince and lover.

MULTIPLE TRIBAL AFFILIATIONS

The corporate archetypes deal with only a narrow band of all possible expressions of the Anima and Animus. There are no children in corporations. Men and women over sixty-five are also excluded. Pre- and post- corporate individuals surely influence what goes on in corporations, but they are peripheral to the main activities.

Many of the ceremonies and events that used to take place in tribes now happen in other settings — births occur in hospitals; naming ceremonies, weddings, and funerals occur in churches or the equivalent — not in corporations.

Modern men and women have *multiple tribal affiliations*, to their nation, their religion, and political party; to their high school and college alumni associations, their professional associations, to various sports teams, to hobby-oriented groups and to families. Since most married couples do not work in the same corporation, each spouse has his or her own set of tribal affiliations and they rarely match up.

In earlier tribal adaptations, all these activities took place within the same cluster of several extended families. As the agricultural era began to spread, several huge ethnic clusters that shared common geography, racial, and religious roots first emerged, and then dispersed across the earth. In his book *Tribes*,[5] Joel Kotkin describes how five such groups, the Jews, the British, the Japanese, the Chinese, and the Indians grew into global tribes which share quintessential characteristics that still bring them success in the economy of the twenty-first century.

Kotkin was using the term *tribes* in a very broad sense. "Tribes" in his sense are clusters of peoples made up of many tribes that share a common kinship and a common culture.

Corporations are special and specific kinds of tribes that are built not around the ties of kinship and shared history but a (sometimes only temporary) shared objective for the present and future: survival and growth. In the first one hundred years of this new mutation, these tribes have developed new food-getting methods and skills.

As the influence of the corporation grows, it is increasingly becoming the primary tribal affiliation for millions of human beings. The bonds of commitment they demand, both economic and emotional, are increasingly suppressing other commitments. The Corporation is actually competing with other tribes, including religions, for the time and allegiance of its employees.

In Japan, weddings are not uncommon corporate ceremonies. In the United States, wedding and baby showers frequently are held inside corporate offices. Corporations are increasingly sponsoring sports teams, hobby groups, even shared vacations among employee groups. Thus, even though the influence of corporations is less complete than the influence of earlier tribal adaptations, it is still profound, and growing.

Unlike earlier tribes, corporations do not require a cradle-to-grave commitment. They deal with only a slice of each individual's life, that portion between college graduation and retirement.

Jung suggested that the unfolding stages of each individuals natural life cycle is archetypal. He defined these stages as "being mothered, exploring the environment, playing in the peer group, adolescence, being initiated, establishing a place in the social hierarchy, courting, marrying, child rearing, hunting, gathering, fighting, participating in religious rituals, assuming the social respon-

---

5. Kotkin, Joel, *Tribes, How Race, Religion, and Identity Determine Success in the New Global Economy* (New York, Random House, 1993).

sibilities of advanced maturity, and preparation for death. Ultimately, every individual life is the same as the eternal life of the species."[6]

Many of the stages that Jung described happen before or after the corporate chapters of our lives. In fact, the only stage Jung listed which occurs during working hours are the food-getting activities, the hunting and gathering, and these occur in a new and different form.

In most industrial societies, the rite of passage that represents what Jung called "being initiated" is the commencement ceremony. It allows young people to join in adult food-getting activities; in fact, the level at which they are recognized at commencement has much to do with the level at which they will be invited to participate in the hunting and gathering. In the modern schema, this rite does not occur within the setting of the new, adult life; it happens in high school and college auditoriums.

Corporate archetypes find expression during the daily food-getting activities of industrialized men and women. The money we work for is a brief intermediary; we are actually working to get food, clothing, entertainment, and all the other symbolic forms of "food" that we consume daily.

By analyzing that part of the human life cycle, and that portion of the daily and weekly activity corporations absorb, it becomes clear that corporations are special and specific kinds of tribes. They have an ancient purpose. The fighting and hunting corporate employees are involved with no longer includes actual bloodshed. It has evolved into fighting for market share within a given territory, and hunting for new customers. Most service activities have clear parallels in the gathering paradigm. *Corporations are essentially hunting and gathering tribes.*

It is clear that the way humans cluster depends to some degree on their food-getting methods and technology. Hunting and gathering is more team oriented than farming and wherever the transition to agriculture occurred, the closely clustered villages of hunters and gatherers spread out. Farmers lived in single family dwellings closer to their crops and their dwellings became more permanent. Team activities still occurred at harvest time, but tribal gatherings and activities became weekly events, in religious centers and village government buildings. On continents where huge areas were converted to crop land, such as Russia, Australia, Argentina, China, South Africa and the United States and

---

6. Jung, Carl G., *The Collected Works of Carl G. Jung*, (London, Routledge & Kegan. Paul; New York: Pantheon, 1962).

Canada, the "rugged individual" could survive and prosper without the need for daily team oriented food-getting activity. In the agricultural era the largest human clusters occurred in organized religions, armies, and governments. Daily food-getting activities were primarily family or individual tasks.

In the context of team activity, corporations, with so many interlocking teams of workers, are more like hunting and gathering tribes than the small family-focused work groups our grandfathers knew. The emergence of corporations involved a return to the team-oriented survival activity of tribes. The typical corporate worker is required to give up some of the independence and autonomy his grandparents enjoyed, and subsume his personal interests and impulses in order to comply with the tribal customs and policies of his or her company. Now, individualism and self-sufficiency can be seen as liabilities; the emphasis is on teamwork and cooperation.

Chapter Two:
Soft- vs. Hard-Style Management

The growing influence of the soft female archetype, the softer approach, is among the most dramatic evolutionary changes coming about as corporate tribes mature. Even our definition of the characteristics of the ideal leader is being softened. The corporate hierarchy was originally modeled on the military. Now, experience has shown that to be firm, powerful and decisive is not always best; being collaborative, participative and nurturing with subordinates is sometimes more effective in getting the desired results. Predatory and ruthless behavior with customers and suppliers ("Get the order and get out"), or driving the vendors' price down as far as possible, may win once; but in the long run it can cost more than forming partnerships that are seen as mutually beneficial. This is an example where the application of the female archetype can get better results.

In boom times, the supply of workers cannot keep up with demand, especially for those with education, training and appropriate skills who are willing to submit to the discipline of corporate life. This makes the soft-style management preferable. Corporations cannot afford to lose good employees. In such a situation, co-option is more efficient than coercion.

Conversely, when the economy is less robust, there is an oversupply of workers which allows corporations to pick and choose the most qualified, while the rest are left in reserve. In such times, a harsher style of management comes into effect, imposed on those lucky ones who still have a job — with longer hours, increased work loads, reduced benefits.

The 1980s and 90s introduced the softer management style, so that the corporate discourse was infused with talk about Anima and the feminine archetype. Books were published and magazines were filled with articles touting the "new" values; everyone was jumping on the bandwagon of the feminization of the social and work relationship. The idea of nurturing everything — employees, customers, even suppliers — and the increasing hesitancy to confront, criticize, discipline, or fire employees are other manifestations.

The current emphasis on Anima is apparent in any bookstore. Simply count the number of books on women's issues compared with men's studies. The awakening of interest in pagan religious ideologies, female gods, and the corresponding questioning of the traditional male god are also indications.

The entire women's movement with all its ramifications may be seen as a burgeoning of Anima in our lifetime. The growing emphasis on women's athletics and the opening of military jobs, the opening of all-male prep schools and social clubs are all geared to preparing more women to join the workforce. Such changes are usually associated with a low unemployment rate and are evidence of an insatiable need for employees at all levels.

As the wars in Afghanistan and Iraq show, these shifts do not guarantee any softening in the approach to major issues. Sometimes, corporate interests are among the basic reasons for declaring war. During good times, corporations persuade everyone that it is in his best interest to be soft and cooperative. When corporations reach the point of conflict among themselves, whether they are fighting over resources, markets or labor, and the conflict is no longer negotiable, then major conflicts erupt across national or international borders. The Civil War in the US was started over irreconcilable interests between the "tribes" of the North and the South. World War I and II, the Cold War and the "war" on terrorism are examples of large-scale international conflagrations over similar irreconcilable corporate interests.

ANIMA AS BREAD WINNER

Within foraging societies, those who gathered have always made immense contributions to the food of their tribes. Martin and Voorhies studied ninety such societies in Africa, Asia, Australia, and the Americas and found that over two-thirds of these tribes rely on products of gathering for 40 to 60% of their diet.[7]

Marjorie Shostak reported in her study of !Kung women that gatherers accounted for 60 to 80% of the total food consumed by weight.[8]

It is instructive to note that even though gatherers play such a major role in feeding the tribe, the hunters usually get more recognition and glory. Elaborate ceremonies and dances often follow the successful hunt. The hunters are honored, sometimes recreating their stalk and recounting the story while all the tribes people celebrate. Of course, hunting and gathering in these tribes breaks down into clear and separate gender roles. Although men sometimes assist in major harvests or in obtaining especially valued foods such as honey, women do most of the gathering. Women may set traps and snares and frequently bring back small animals as well as birds and fish.

There are a few examples of women who hunt. Tiwi women, who live on Melville Island off the northern coast of Australia, hunt with dogs; and among some tribes of the Agta of Northeastern Luzon, women use bows and arrows to hunt pigs, deer, and monkeys. But the bulk of animal protein is provided by men and the killing of big game is universally assigned to men.

It may be more important to observe the tremendous variations in food-getting techniques practiced in tribal societies than to limit attention to the most obvious and always-mentioned separation of gender roles. The ability of humankind to vary their hunting and gathering methods (sometimes working alone, sometimes in small parties, sometimes with entire tribes including children, sometimes even combining the human resources of several related tribes) may represent a more important observation. Coastal tribes in Hawaii and Polynesia often convoked huge gatherings of tribes people to surround fish, and then beat the water and drive them into nets. African Pygmies employ very similar techniques, often joining with several tribes to surround a patch of forest and drive animals into nets. Similar strategies were used by Plains Indians to drive buffalo herds off cliffs. The particular composition of a food-getting team depended on the game, the terrain, and the beliefs and customs of a tribe as well

---

7. Martin, Kay M. and Voorhies, Barbara, op. cit.
8. Shostak, Marjorie, *NISA, The Life and Words of a !Kung Woman* (New York: Random House, Inc. 1981).

as on the strategy and available human resources. No other species employs this kind of versatility.

In foraging tribes, gatherers also collected intelligence about food supplies. When large game animals were encountered during gathering activities, the hunters were alerted. Perhaps more critical, when enemy hunters were discovered within a tribe's hunting territory, reports of their numbers and activities were passed to the hunters.

The knowledge and experience required to be a successful gatherer was at least as complex and challenging as that required for successful hunting. Where hunters tried to understand the habits and movements of prey, gatherers had to recognize plants, where edible roots might be found beneath the ground, and where and when a harvest of nuts, berries or vegetables would be ready. The location of potent medicinal herbs, knowledge of poisons, and methods for making foods edible had to be carefully mastered and passed down generation after generation in order to assure a tribe's survival.

Tribal Day Care

Child rearing has always been blended with the activities of gathering. In many tribes a sort of day care arrangement was common where a few of the gatherers would remain in camp to care for small or sick children. The practice of carrying children into the field was typical and widespread. They rested in sacks and on cradle boards, sometimes hung from tree branches when the foraging work got heavy. Infants spent a major chunk of their waking hours in physical contact with their mothers.

Ten thousand years ago, when the knowledge of agriculture began to drive such profound changes in the lives and cultures of humankind, the nurturing skills of gatherers were turned toward the growing of crops and the tending and care of domestic animals. These roles were less gender-specific. They often involved both men and women. The hunting and war activities of men became part time and the nurturing required to tend crops and animals may have been early influences that helped to modify and blend gender roles. The role of the farmer's wife, as recently as two generations ago, frequently included planting, tending and harvesting a vegetable garden, and raising chickens, pigs and milk cows; while male roles, as in hunting and gathering tribes, required travel away from home to tend larger herds or to plant and harvest larger plots.

Agriculture forced a breakdown in the large extended family structures of hunting and gathering tribes. As family clusters disbursed more thinly across crop producing territory, large group activities became less frequent. In this situation, communal day care was less practical.

It is important to note that agricultural women were also bread winners. As was the case with tribal gatherers, they contributed a major share of the food and sustenance for their families. In this broader historical context it is clear that the early period of industrialization, when many women were not expected to be breadwinners, was a hiatus, and the massive inflow of women to the corporate work force is a recovery of the natural order.

Another frequent activity of gatherers has to do with handwork. In all cultures forms of handwork requiring very fine motor coordination — weaving, beadwork, knitting, sewing, braiding of hair, working of clay, and the preparation of food and clothing — were frequent occupations of gatherers. Here, too, there are great overlaps. Men also worked with their hands in ways that required skill and dexterity; but hunters were more frequently involved in the manufacture of weapons, fishing nets, canoes, and large structures where strength was a factor.

Chapter Three:
Gathering in Corporate Tribes

Like in any tribe, the hunters have their irreplaceable roles, and so do the gathering groups. Most of the gathering activities that used to exist in tribes still exist, in evolved form, in modern corporations. Furthermore, when these functions are performed well, they have an immense impact on the bottom line. They are not at all difficult to identify and locate. Just look for where most of the jobs are still performed by large groups of women. Perhaps the classic data entry department is the most obvious example. Telemarketing and customer service functions which often involve huge banks of telephones are largely staffed by women. Airline reservation agents provide a classic example as do the telephone sales agents in travel companies and those who staff the 800 numbers of major hotel chains.

Also, modern tests of fine motor skills show that women generally are more dexterous than men. Corporations that manufacture computer chips and miniature electronic equipment take this into account by staffing their assembly lines almost entirely with women.

In all corporations, accounts receivable can be seen as a key gathering function. Collecting money, pulling together invoices efficiently so that the corporate tribe can sustain the cash flow it needs to operate, is like the harvesting of crops, like gleaning, like collecting food in the bush.

Corporate gathering functions normally involve some form of nurturing, such as human resources, training and development, and customer services.

A skilled gatherer can be most effective in a customer service role. Some telephone sales professionals function almost like beaters, moving out ahead of the hunters to scare up game. They develop leads. Others, as in the case of airline or hotel reservations agents, account for a very high percentage of a corporation's revenues, far more than the field sales force.

In a great many industries, the field sales representative establishes a relationship or gets a contract, but the orders against that contract are taken over the telephone by gatherers. Careful analysis reveals that what the sales person sold and what was ultimately delivered are often very different. A skilled and aggressive gatherer can often ship more than was originally ordered. By establishing a nurturing relationship with the customer, a skilled gatherer can create an ongoing partnership that can last for years. In tribal terms, this process can be seen as domesticating the tribal herd.

Conversely, poor gathering can turn a great sale into something less. A partner of a major consulting firm sold a series of six training programs to a new client, a large manufacturing firm. Once the initial sale was confirmed, the project was turned over to a project manager who in turn involved a gatherer, a client relations manager, to work with the client's human resources people to identify and schedule the attendees. The first two sessions went as planned. However, the client requested some format changes prior to the third session and when several attendees canceled at the last minute, the session was delayed. After two months, the third session got off the ground but the consulting firm had assigned a new trainer who was not totally familiar with the material and feedback from the client was not as good. Then, too, the session ran with three fewer attendees than was planned. After that, the project more or less withered on the vine. Enthusiasm had waned. Both the consulting firm and the client were focused on different priorities.

This story is familiar to all companies. Once the hunter brings down a buffalo, do the gatherers take only the tongue and hindquarters and leave the rest to rot? Companies are looking for gatherers who get it all. A skilled team, one that knows what its doing, can actually bring the animal back alive, nurture it, make it healthy, and take a harvest of its milk or wool day after day, year after year.

Chapter Three: Gathering in Corporate Tribes

GATHERING AS SHOPPING

The trade and barter for food and manufactured items is an obvious precursor to activities that have come into full bloom with corporate tribes. The actual activity of gathering for modern men and women has a new name. We call it shopping. The entire field of retailing can be seen as an elaborate and massive evolution of the gathering role.

One clue to this concept is that in retailing, the customer comes to the store. In this sense the store can be seen as an elaborate trap. The window displays are a form of bait, designed to attract attention. The customer and sales clerk perform a kind of ritual, and if the goods are appealing and the clerk says the right words, a transaction occurs.

The shopping mall, and the dense collection of downtown stores are the evolved orchards, fields, and forests (and often have literally replaced them, on the ground) where gatherers go during the day. These became farmers' markets during the agricultural era, places where cloth, beads, and manufactured objects, as well as food, were traded. In our era they have blossomed into dazzling bazaars, a paradise for the serious "shop till you drop" gatherer. In the typical modern supermarket, the gathering has never been better. One can find strawberries from Chile in January, fresh fish thousands of miles from the ocean, cheeses of every variety from all over the world, wines from France, Australia, and South Africa; coffees, tobaccos, chocolate; the choices and variety boggle the mind. Roll the clock back, and no king or sultan had the great luxury of choices we take so much for granted. In order to enjoy something as commonplace as ice, the Czar of Russia had to dispatch a train to Siberia. Oranges were such a rare luxury that Louis XVI ordered trees imported for his palace at Versailles.

There may be a gender difference in the appetite for shopping that can be traced back to our hunting and gathering roots. Simple observation might suggest that women enjoy this activity more and spend more time doing it than men. The skill sets of a good gatherer may be similar to those of a good shopper. The ability to remember where nuts or berries can be found and how to determine when roots are ready for harvesting may parallel a modern gatherer's knowledge of sales, coupon redemptions, and special deals. Some observers have indicated the women are more patient comparison shoppers than men. They may enjoy simply wandering about in the neon forest to see what they can see, what they need, what looks good. Men, on the other hand, typically decide they need a new pair of socks when a hole appears in an old pair. They go to the store with a specific mission, walk straight to the sock counter, oblivious to the sale signs around them, make their purchase, and leave. The sock is like a deer or a rabbit, something to hunt for.

If gathering involves searching for things, in bookcases, computers, files or drawers, conventional wisdom suggests that women are more skilled than men. When car keys or cuff links disappear, a woman can often go through a drawer searched minutes before by her husband and find them.

Like retail services, the entire food services industry has evolved from the nurturing aspect of the Anima archetype. From grandma's chicken soup to dishing up meals for the masses in university cafeterias and airlines in-flight services, providing nourishment is classical Anima.

Feeding and watering people is another large-scale "gathering" function and the millions of employees who staff these modern feeding stations must follow the basic rules of all gatherers. They must be fast, friendly, and efficient in dispensing the burgers and gathering in the money.

Because they are essentially providing a service, all hotels, resorts, inns or other purveyors of hospitality are staffed primarily by gatherer-types. To the extent that these gatherers understand their role and are able to display nurturing in their relationships with customers, their business is likely to be successful.

Because all hospitals, nursing homes, clinics, and other health care organizations deal with healing and the preservation of life, they can be said to draw on the Anima archetype. In the early stage of the industrial revolution, nursing represented one of the most common avenues for women who wanted professional careers, and it still provides a natural fit for individuals, whether men or women, who are nurturing by nature.

All education draws on the characteristics attributed to the Anima archetype. It is therefore not surprising to see such a heavy concentration of women, particularly in the primary grades, in this profession. It comes to many of them naturally.

Recognizing the relationship between nurturing and services empowers corporate gatherers. Nurturing, the desire to make things grow, the tendency to take time to tend living things, to ease distress, to give food, warmth, comfort, and care are fundamental expression of Anima, the female archetype.

Nurturing represents an active ingredient in all successful relationships, especially with children, but also with employees, colleagues, and customers of the corporate tribe. In families, nurturing is the fundamental element of the mothering role.

Nurturing in Corporations

In most corporations, the expression of nurturing is greatly diluted. Open displays of affection are essentially taboo and the kindly manager who puts his or her arm around an employee, even with wholesome intentions, can be accused of sexual harassment.

Nurturing, in its diluted corporate form, is expressed as encouragement, praise, and recognition. As noted above, it is fundamental to all training, teaching, and instruction. It finds powerful expression in coaching and mentoring relationships.

In *Iron John*, Robert Bly describes mentoring as "taking an employee into your heart."[9] It involves a serious time commitment as well as an emotional investment. Some corporations have instituted formal mentoring programs where employees are assigned to mentors, but these are only marginally successful. Some employees are too proud or prickly to attract a mentor. A significant number of corporate employees go through their entire careers without ever being mentored. Some psychologists have even suggested that children who grow up without fathers, or with alcoholic or emotionally unstable fathers, are less successful in attracting mentors. Those employees who somehow remind an executive of a son or daughter, even on a subconscious level, are more successful in attracting mentors. It may be that employees who had nurturing fathers and mothers are more inclined to seek out mentors than those who did not.

It is unlikely that the nurturing instinct is evenly distributed among women. That distribution, like so many other human traits, probably follows a normal curve. By the same token, some men are naturally more inclined to be nurturing than others.

Sometimes, people get stuck playing roles they would rather avoid. A woman professor of Sociology at a major university, a Ph.D., found that her motherly appearance drew students to her in a way that ate up all her time and kept her from her research work. Her greying hair, kindly smile, and the twinkle

---

9. Bly, Robert, *Iron John* (New York: Addison-Wesley Publishing Company, Inc. 1990).

in her eye were so instantly familiar that a steady flow of needy, lonely students were drawn to her like moths to a flame. She could hardly walk down a corridor at the university without attracting some childlike freshman yearning for some reassuring milk of human kindness. She was exhausted. Whenever she attempted to rebuff such advances, she felt guilty; and if she let down her guard, even slightly, she had students pouring out their most intimate life stories, expecting her to help them. The image she projected was deceptive. Tests revealed that she was an introvert. She loved research, ideas, science, theories and concepts. She had dutifully raised two of her own children, patiently setting aside her passion for research. She had expected that when they became adults she could, at last, follow her dream. That time had come and gone, and she still felt trapped in a nurturing role than had long ago lost its savor.

Her story shows that we have an inborn response to a certain image as the nurturer, the care-giver. Sculptured images and icons of fertility goddesses and earth mothers have been unearthed in archeological digs from various cultures, and the image strikes even modern men and women as both familiar and powerful. It pulls almost everyone, at some deep subconscious level, back to the post-womb hours of nursing and skin-to-skin contact with someone large and warm and safe, someone with big loving eyes. These experiences, largely preconscious, occur in the first two years of life before words and memory develop.

There is some evidence that infants who get a full measure of nurturing in these early stages develop a foundation of confidence in the stability and predictability of the world that allows for later exploratory behavior. Conversely, disruption or inadequate doses of this primary nurturing may create a constant unrelenting effort to control an unpredictable and irrational world in order to achieve an enduring level of safety and security. In his most famous study, Harlow[10] discovered that monkeys raised with wire mothers, rather than cloth ones, explored their environment less. This suggests that the power of Anima is rooted in more than food, breasts and mother's milk. It is also skin contact. It is life giving. It creates confidant adults.

In *The Chalice and the Blade*,[11] Riane Eisler makes the intriguing assertion that pre-hunting, pre-war humans were nurturing, creative, caring and compas-

---

10. Harlow, Harry F., in *Principles of General Psychology* (New York: John Wiley and Sons, 1980).
11. Eisler, Riane, *The Chalice & The Blade, Our History, Our Future* (San Francisco: HarperCollins Publishers, Inc. 1987).

sionate by nature and that the bloodshed, cruelty and domination of warlike people who worshiped the power of the blade was a later, perhaps temporary, stage of man's evolutionary development. It is not difficult to picture early men and women as foragers, rather than hunters, as benign and nurturing as mountain gorillas. In early stages of development, when populations of Homo sapiens were sparse and edible foods plentiful, reasons for conflict such as competition for food providing territory must have been much less urgent. Who can say when the appetite for meat arose and when foraging societies added hunting to their food-getting activities? It is refreshing to consider the possibility that the model of dominance, conquest, and bloody competition for hunting grounds and cropland may be a throwback to a temporary chapter in human evolution that is otherwise driven by the nurturing power of Anima.

A corporation with an impressive customer service function almost lost everything when it "fixed" something that wasn't broken. The corporation was selling all of its products through large, independently-owned truck dealerships. It had about 450 clearly defined customers. This customer "herd" grew slowly, since the market was fairly mature. The primary growth came through the introduction of new products. The quality of the services the corporation provided to its key customers was critical since their competition was always alert and ready to move in. The customer service staff was far more integrated into the company's manufacturing and inventory functions than in the typical corporation. They took an active role in forecasting production and inventory requirements on the basis of orders and contracts they administered. They helped the company clear out inventory when an old product had been discontinued. They took part in discussions and planning of new products, contributing information gleaned from their customer contacts. Although the head of the customer service group was a man, all but one of the representatives were seasoned females. They averaged about eight years of service. The company seemed most vulnerable to losing customers when the person on the other end of the telephone line changed. This, of course, disrupted the working relationship the customer service person had worked so hard to establish.

Perhaps the management team should have been more attentive to this clue before deciding to reorganize. Instead of giving each customer service professional her own list of dealers, it was decided that they should reorganize by products. Unwittingly, their reorganization concept disrupted many delicate working relationships that had taken months, sometimes years, to build. Now, several representative were calling the same purchasing person, each pushing different products.

Within a few months, a negative jolt in sales and complaints from customers confirmed what the customer service people had said from the beginning. The reorganization had blurred the focus on the customer and strained the quality of long-established working relationships. When the company reversed its reorganization and returned to its prior system, sales gradually returned to normal.

Anima and Corporate Profits

Those corporations who understand the archetypal roles should hire people with a strong natural gathering and nurturing tendency for service positions and concentrate the hunter-types on "bagging" new business. Still, the vast majority of corporations make the same mistakes as all male-dominated tribes: they admire, promote, and pay their hunters well, while under-estimating, under-employing, under-training, and underpaying their gatherers. They seem to regard customer service jobs as simple, entry level positions and they tend to hire young, inexperienced workers to fill them. They have no systems to track the results of their gatherers. They do not provide quality training in how to be an effective gatherer, nor do they offer bonuses to reward the best performers. Gathering jobs are undervalued and, indeed, are a missed opportunity to boost the bottom line.

Millions of dollars in sales can be lost if the customer service people are not able to turn customer calls into actual orders, if they are not able to collect on everything that the sales people sold, or if they see contacts with customers as single discreet events rather than relationship building. For these reasons, corporations need to focus on training and measuring the performance of employees in positions that are often considered low priority.

Even major firms do not necessarily understand the distinction between hunting and gathering roles within their own organization. When they find promising young recruits, they often assign them to positions that are patently unsuited to their abilities. More than one young man has been hired because he was sharp and eager, aggressive, and competitive, but then found himself assigned to a job that required a talent for nurturing. Rather than recognize, develop, and use his hunting capabilities and temperament, for example, he might be assigned to a gathering job selling products over the telephone.

In their personal lives, such men keep their telephone calls short and sweet; they rarely call anyone just to chat. They soon find they have a difficult time selling products. They may present the products clearly but move too quickly to try to take the order, leaving customers feeling pressured and uncomfortable. Then, seeing that others are making more sales than they are, they become frustrated and their competitive juices tell them that something is wrong — so that it is even more difficult to relax and keep a telephone conversation going. Often, within a few months, they quit in frustration and find that their career has already gotten off on a sour note. Many of them would have performed much better as field sales representatives.

Few corporations understand the gathering role. They and the employees generally see customer service as "being nice to customers." The corporation would seek, instead, to have customer service employees adopt the perspective of bringing in revenues, making sales, in short — feeding their tribe.

Corporations can consciously play on the gatherer archetype to strengthen their professional gatherers' contribution to the bottom line. Working this archetype may influence how they select, train, and reward those who fulfill this role.

What Makes a Good Corporate Gatherer

When headhunters, employment agencies and human resources departments understand the different archetypal food-getting roles, they screen and sort job applicants accordingly. Good shoppers, bargain hunters, employees eager to find a good deal are likely to have a general inclination toward 'gathering" activities. When interviewers ask, "Do you have a green thumb?" "Do you have pets?" and "Who takes care of and feeds the pets?" they are probing to see whether the interviewee is nurturing by nature.

If they are consciously looking to utilize the "anima" paradigm, they screen for applicants who love children, are good cooks and like to feed and entertain others. Interviewers filling customer service positions want to hear that the applicant has a lot of friends, is popular and gregarious, and enjoys talking on the telephone. Chatting with the customer will come naturally to them, and they will be able to keep up a cheerful demeanor without getting impatient. Those who enjoy being mothers do well in gathering roles, especially when they can transfer their nurturing temperaments to their internal and external customers.

Of course, to get the most out of these employees, it is also critical for management and the field sales force to understand the fundamental principle. When customer service employees are no longer passive order takers and clerical workers waiting for their next paycheck but are expected to perform as true corporate gatherers, they produce greater results. Studying how gatherers functioned in earlier tribes can be a valuable element of their training.

Some tribal analogies make the pattern clear. For example:

- *Customers are the tribal herd.* The herd must be fed, and if they don't like what they get, they are likely to be lured away by a tribe that feeds them better. In the corporate scenario, what the herd wants is good information as well as quality products and services that arrive on time and are exactly what was ordered.
- It is easier to milk the cow when it recognizes the milk maid's voice, and when the milkmaid calls out its name. *Developing a first-name relationship* is an important element in building and maintaining a strong customer service bond. The "pros" in every field know how essential it is to develop a first-name relationship with the President's secretary. Since she or he schedules appointments and helps the boss keep track of activities, the secretary is a critical gatekeeper.
- It works even better if the sales and service people have met the customer face to face. Corporations understand that this is an important way to increase the quality of the bond, and inspire some loyalty from the customer.
- Forward-thinking companies even invite key customers to some of their team-building seminars and activities, not to mention the holiday party. If they can get even the customers to see themselves as part of, or affiliates to, the corporation then they are far ahead in the game.
- Protecting the herd from predators is important to any company. If gatherers can be trained to sniff out when someone else is feeding or milking their cows, the hunters can be alerted. Redoubled efforts on the part of the sales agents, special offers and other ploys will be brought to bear and convince the client not to stray.
- *Understanding the needs and habits of the herd* is also critical. Successful companies find out what foods they like, when they like to be milked, what things upset them or undermine their contentment. Clients that feel good about how they are treated are the easiest ones to milk.

It may seem demeaning to see a corporation's customers as the tribal herd. They could as well be compared to a crop that must be tended and nurtured.

Either way, the smart corporations know (consciously or unconsciously) what kind of people to place in client-contact positions.

The earlier and more primitive goals of the hunter did not involve relationship building, and in some businesses, one-time selling opportunities still replicate that model. Like hunters, some modern salesmen and women focus only on getting the sale, and for them, it is like making a kill. In most cases, however, there is some chance of developing follow-up sales and so the most successful are those who cultivate their "prey."

How to Reward Corporate Gatherers

Increasingly, companies are tracking employee performance in an effort to get the best output for the least investment. Corporations that really want to spur their customer service representatives to do more than just take whatever comes in over the telephone are learning to measure the success rate of these gatherers, and reward them accordingly. While it is easier to measure the sales generated by the hunters, in-house sales staff often can expand an order by introducing new products or services, or by offering specials. If they can reduce the inventory of obsolete products, get customers to try new products, generate leads that become sales, or take an active role in renewing and expanding contracts, then the dollars they generate for their companies are no different than other sales dollars.

Which sales approach produces the best results is sometimes surprising A regional airline offers a good illustration. Its hunter warriors were the pilots, still wearing military-like uniforms with stripes on the sleeves and emblems on the hats that denoted status in the dominance hierarchy. Its troops were the mechanics and baggage handlers. As with all airlines, its gatherers were ticket and gate agents, and the reservation agents. When they computerized the telephones in their ticket sales area, for the first time they could measure how many calls each agent took, the total dollars in ticket sales each agent generated, the amount of time that passed between calls, and the amount of time spent on the telephone with each customer.

They were surprised to discover large differences in productivity and even more surprised to learn that the most experienced and senior level agents, who were also highest paid, were often least productive. Looking into this further, they discovered that the most productive agents were not the most intelligent.

In fact, high intelligence contributed to higher turnover. Apparently, more intelligent and better-educated agents became bored quickly and found it difficult to remain focused and interested in the constant and unremitting stream of telephone calls. The best, most productive agents were less educated but they enjoyed being helpful to customers and solving their travel problems, and were able to maintain a cheerful and helpful attitude even after several hours.

Without further milking the client cow metaphor, some of these same basic concepts can also be applied to other gathering functions, for example to the employment, training and development of a tribe's human resources. This is clearly a nurturing function. The challenge of searching for, screening, hiring and then training and developing a corporation's human resources in a way that yields a clear advantage over competitors requires care, technical knowledge, patience, and skill that is similar to and every bit as demanding as planting, tending and raising a healthy crop.

Just as a clumsy gardener can cut down a healthy plant along with the weeds, so also can a clumsy manager dash the morale and energetic participation of a young and growing employee. By the same token, an astute manager can induce employees to feel that fulfilling the company objectives is the same as fulfilling their own personal objectives, and that excelling at the company is the same as excelling in life.

Employees that are fed with good information can be groomed to become mature, seasoned corporate hunters and gatherers. Corporations rely on them to pass on knowledge of the tribe's unique products, selling techniques, markets, and customers to each new generation. Those who fail to retain their experienced staff incur the need to train new people constantly, which is costly in every sense.

In the major gathering function known as accounts receivable, the speed with which corporate billings are collected relates directly to the experience, talent and skill of the gatherers assigned to this function. Companies that apply the techniques of pre-billing or collecting a chunk of the billings up front, of calling the accounts payable person by name and developing a reliable flow of payments on the basis of a good working relationship are stronger than those who let the bill collectors see their jobs as a clerical activity.

Entry level positions for gatherers are often include clerical and secretarial jobs as well as receptionist positions. They, too, can be made to contribute to the bottom-line success of an organization by applying archetypal gathering skills.

Here, nurturing takes the form of building relationships with internal and external customers, greeting visitors to the tribal compound, screening and scheduling appointments and telephone calls, searching the bushes for files and information, using fine motor skills for typing and computer entry, and yes, providing coffee. While asking someone to bring coffee is sometimes done as a way of showing dominance, the act of serving it is a classical nurturing activity that helps generate a welcoming, comfortable atmosphere.

In modern corporations, nurturers sometimes express their instinct by informally feeding the tribe — this includes the cookies, cakes, and treats that they often bring in spontaneously, especially during holidays and tribal celebrations. Such voluntary feeding is powerful proof that this innate drive exists and can be tapped for corporate benefit.

The Velvet Carpet

Some gatherers have more power in their tribes (and corporations) than an outsider might guess. Their power may not be clear on the organization chart, the formal dominance hierarchy, but runs parallel to it. On the other hand, every executive understands the power of the boss's secretary or administrative assistant. Perhaps some attention should be given to the "velvet carpet": executives have it yanked out from under them when they ignore or fail to appreciate or show deference to a high-ranking corporate gatherer.

The president usually relies on his administrative assistant as a sharp and astute gatekeeper. The person holding this position is more powerful, more experienced and better paid than the administrative assistants of Vice Presidents. He or she can control the agenda of meetings as well as who gets access to the boss. Understanding the informal power and authority of top level gatherers, and learning how to work within the appropriate boundaries, is essential for all corporate employees. Like the glass ceiling, the velvet carpet is subtle and difficult for the naive corporate employee to deal with and negotiate.

Some recent research has suggested that women are more collaborative in their basic approach to leadership and problem solving than men. It has been suggested that they are less concerned about hierarchy and less inclined to rely on position power to get things done. However, it should be noted that in all large corporations, the female pecking order is clear to the females who occupy the top rungs. Women executives know who is the top ranking, top paid, "highest level" female in their company.

It is instructive to note that in all-female organizations, such as some of the more prestigious women's universities in the United States, one finds the same dominance hierarchies as in any other large human organization. They have a university president, deans and department heads, tenured and untenured professors — essentially a replica of other universities. The fact that all jobs in these universities may be performed by women, right down to mowing the lawns and repairing the furnaces, shows that women can and do perform any and all jobs. However, the essential point is that women clearly understand dominance hierarchies and, in fact, create them when they have to decide how to organize in all-female organizations.

The concept of male bonding can be threatening to capable women executives who are not invited or have no interest in golf outings or discussions of football game; but they may find ways of winning inclusion where it counts. Women, too, usually form cooperative networks, hold private meetings, and take an active role in promoting policies and programs that will help their causes, and high-level female executives often identify and form mentoring bonds with high potential younger women.

VULNERABILITIES AND BLIND SPOTS

The nurturing of the gatherer is a powerful element in all service-oriented professions and corporations; of course, the more nurturing individuals are, the less likely they are to be effective when toughness or ruthlessness is necessary and appropriate. When it comes to closing a sale, firing an employee, demanding excellence from employees, being firm and direct with problem performers, asking for a raise or disputing an invoice, they are likely to be uncomfortable if not ineffective.

For this reason, nurturing managers and executives may be at a disadvantage in the competition for internal resources. They may find it extremely difficult to hold firmly to their demand for more space, more people, more equipment and a larger share of the corporate budget. Insisting on anything, and entering into confrontation, are just too distressing for people who are inclined to be nice, kind, cooperative, and helpful.

A nurturer/gatherer may be more interested in harmony and a comfortable nest than in capturing, expanding and defending territory, even when that territory is a prime corner office.

The primary vulnerabilities of gatherers often occur when their nurturance is engaged. Some employees know how to play this vulnerability like a fiddle: "I know the target date for the report I am working on is today, but my six-year-old daughter is having her first piano recital, and I feel I must be there. I hope you understand." Faced with this excuse, a nurturing manager is likely to melt.

Super nurturing managers may mother-hen their employees and try to protect them from the unrelenting demands of those hard-hearted Vice Presidents who think of nothing but profits. In some cases, they may prefer good morale and a heart-to-heart chat about a personal problem to high levels of productivity. Corporate warriors think lean and mean, and hold employees accountable for their performance or nonperformance; gatherers more often try to solve performance problems with more nurturing. They may coach and mentor, month after month, and then feel personally responsible when employees do not respond or do not perform as needed.

Where do we draw the line between appropriate support and sensitivity, and tolerating outright nonperformance? One manager was editing a report that had been written by a young staff assistant who happened to be in her seventh month of pregnancy. The report was poorly done; in fact, it had to be completely redone. It was copied so carelessly from another document that it still contained the name of the wrong company. Yet, when the boss explained what was needed and asked her to do it over, the woman broke into tears and rushed out of the office; the manager was soon called into his boss's office and roundly criticized for being insensitive.

By the same token, an employee who tries to focus on the need to increase billable time or point out ways in which other firms are more profitable may be criticized as being too competitive. Where is the right balance? Any tribe needs some of each type, in order to weather the storms and come out ahead.

Corporations provide a new type of human cluster that does more to blend gender roles than prior tribal forms. There are women who can and do perform all corporate jobs as well as men, and many men have the nurturance required to be effective gatherers. Many women have the toughness and competitive drive to demand excellence from employees, wrestle market share from competitors, and push through unfriendly acquisitions. The days of refusing to give field sales jobs to women because they involve heavy travel are fading. As increasing numbers of women become active in athletics and develop their strength, endurance, and competitive spirit, the line which once resulted in separate and distinct gender roles continues to fade.

CHAPTER FOUR:
ON THE EVOLUTION OF ANIMUS

It is always the male deer, rams, elk, buffalo and elephants who lock horns or tusks and compete for females. The sword play of young men in the dueling fraternities of Europe were embarrassingly similar. In his book *The Cultivation of Hatred*,[12] Peter Gay reminds us that dueling societies were widespread only 150 years ago. Male fraternities in Germany operated with obsessively detailed sets of rules regulating dress, mannerisms, drinking sprees, courtship, and reasons for feeling affronted, as well as dueling procedures and ethics. Dueling involved a ritualized series of steps; an insult, a challenge, selection of a second, selection of weapons, agreement on a time and place, and a woman offstage weeping and wringing her hands.

Anyone who has read *Barbarians at the Gate*[13] will be amazed at what corporate executives can get up to in their pursuit of dominance and displays of power; but even though the stakes were high during the acquisition of Burrough, RJR Nabisco, no one was physically hurt.

Traditional means of defending the tribe's interests, territories, and resources are being replaced or supplemented by more abstract means of asserting control. For the first time in anthropological history, the vast majority of humans may be able to live their entire lives without personally killing an

---

12. Gay, Peter, *The Cultivation of Hatred, The Bourgeois Experience, Victoria to Freud* (London: W. W. Norton & Company, 1993).
13. Bryan & Helyar, John, *Barbarians at the Gate, The Fall of RJR Nabisco* (New York: HarperCollins Publishers 1990).

enemy tribesperson or being killed by one. While people in many parts of the world still live under the very real threat of a bloody war, those living in the most developed nations seem to be spared direct involvement. Corporate competition, competition on the economic plane, is a weapon that allows most of us to keep our hands clean; and smaller, elite battle groups using unmanned drones and long-distance weapons spare even many military recruits from direct combat. There could hardly be a more profound change in the Animus archetype.

Warriors, Infanticide, and Cannibalism

Recent studies of higher mammals are yielding results that are deeply insulting to our self image as Homo sapiens. Adult male lions and tigers systematically kill cubs of competing males when they gain control of a pride. Male bear cubs are also vulnerable and require extra fierce protection from their mothers in order to survive attacks by adult males. During daylight hours, adult male chimpanzees patrol the boundaries of their territories and attack intruders, sometimes killing them — especially infants. And, apparently, this kind of chimpanzee behavior is considered a model of how Homo sapiens behaved during the hunting and gathering stages of evolution.

Infanticide and genocide may have been relatively common until very recently (just read Shakespeare); the relatively frequent accounts of infants being "accidentally" killed by boyfriends or stepfathers suggest that some forms of infanticide may continue to smolder in the animal recesses of our brains. Disturbingly ruthless acts may still be part of the unconscious animal baggage we all carry. It has now been documented that some form of cannibalism existed on almost every continent. It was often conducted as a part of some religious or tribal ceremony, but not always.

The high incidence of rape following military conquest may also hint at a biological drive to spread the DNA of the most successful. The so-called "sperm competition" studies suggest that a survival-of-the-fittest principle may even be functioning in the behavior of human and animal sperm! Female chimpanzees mate with several males during their periods of estrus. It is now theorized that some sperm of the first mate line the fallopian tube and function as guards or soldiers to interrupt, block, kill or slow down the sperm of subsequent competing suitors. Are sperm like colonizing insects with some acting as soldiers, some as drones, and some preserved and protected like a queen bee? Every time science peels back another layer of evolutionary knowledge, we see things that disturb us and run counter to our sublime image of ourselves.

THE NEW WARRIORS

The stunning contracts of professional athletes demonstrate how powerfully the warrior archetype still operates in modern societies. The plumes and shining armor of medieval knights have evolved into high-tech football helmets and shock resistant shoulder pads. The strutting general with a chest full of medals, the big-name tennis star who tosses his sweaty shirt to screaming teenage admirers, the police officer festooned with billy clubs, handcuffs, .38 caliber revolvers, walkie-talkies and a shiny badge: all express something deep and ancient in the fundamental nature of males — and how we respond to them — in our species.

The same paradigm shows up in different environments. In the countryside, it's not uncommon to meet good-hearted, thoughtful, hard-working and intelligent men who are fascinated with guns and who fantasize about being attacked by hippies or criminals: they seem to secretly long for the moment when their masculinity is challenged and all their preparations and target practice are put to the test. Some keep a loaded .44 under the driver's seat of the pickup and a shotgun, also loaded, leaning against the wall next to the front door, "for protection." Millions of men entertain similar violent fantasies. In martial arts classes, in the military, at the shooting range, in prison guard towers and police squad cars, watching wrestling or boxing matches, while sharpening knives or cleaning guns, they dream about what they will do and how the warrior within them will respond in the event of a life-and-death confrontation.

All of us know this warrior archetype, even though we may have difficulty articulating it. We watch with rapt attention as Clint Eastwood, John Wayne, Bruce Willis, Eddie Murphy, Harrison Ford and hundreds of others replay the same cherished mythology, saving the world from evil bad guys. Typically, these heroes endure great pain, quarrel with their authority figure bosses, protect women and children, and always overcome tremendous odds. In the end, they slay the cruel enemy, criminal, traitor, dragon, vampire or alien. They are strong, brave, honest, and good but also have a ruthless streak which allows them to kill. Sonny Bono, Jesse Ventura, Arnold Schwarzenegger, and Ronald Reagan have demonstrated that show business heroes with name recognition can transition into political leadership roles, even without experience in politics. Seeing them on the big screen, playing roles that mesmerize the audience, can obviously be translated into votes.

Athletics provide expressions of the warrior archetype. Warriors must develop their strength through exercise, so they run, lift weights, and practice their evolved swordplay with various racquets, bats, golf clubs, and hockey sticks. Those who excel receive great praise and admiration from their tribes, whether they be schools, nations or cities. They are our modern gladiators.

Not only is our admiration of great athletes, jet fighter pilots, and TV cops and cowboys an indication of the immense power of the warrior archetype, the hours modern men and women spend watching modified war rituals such as football and soccer games on TV further emphasizes the point. How is it possible that an activity which provides no apparent survival advantage consumes so many millions of spectator hours? When one considers the wild headdresses and war painted faces on the more exuberant football fans, and the occasional brawls that break out between opposing spectators, the reality that major sports events are evolved tribal war rituals becomes more clear.

The Warrior Fire and Teenage Crime

Young men everywhere feel the fire of their warriorhood about the time their testosterone starts kicking in. Their desire to fight, to compete, to display their fierceness, to be the admired hero, all begin to flare as their muscles mature, they get taller and their increasing physical strength allows them to do things that they could never do before.

In most tribal societies, adults provide structured adult supervised activities that help young men become hunters and warriors. Between the times of childhood and marriage, young men from several African tribes such as the Masai form warrior societies and take on the responsibility of protecting the tribe and their herds from enemies. In agrarian societies, young men often received their first horse and took on adult responsibility for raising and tending animals following their rite of passage.

Many young men, and young women as well, are proud to recall being given serious responsibility at an early age. Many of our fathers and grandfathers received their first rifles and hunting knives from their fathers. Often these symbols of manhood were passed down from one generation to the next like other family heirlooms. These gifts were usually accompanied by lessons and instructions about safety and the responsible use of weapons.

Cub Scouts, Boy Scouts, Future Farmers of America, ROTC as well as a dazzling array of sports activities and church-sponsored youth programs show that modern societies provide adult supervised developmental programs which are very similar to those observed in hunting and gathering societies.

The Army, Navy, and Marines are logical institutions for aspiring warriors. But huge numbers of young men are left out. The days when judges gave young criminals the choice of going to jail or going into the military are gone. The military no longer accepts them. Modern societies often do not offer sufficient or proper outlets to channel their aggressive drives appropriately. Many have no father at hand, or the father lacks the wisdom and maturity to guide them. The models they see on TV and in movies give all the wrong signals. Quentin Terintino's recent film *Kill Bill* provides a few minutes of adolescent plot, and hours of chopping off arms, legs, and heads complete with fountains of gushing blood. The warrior boastings of teenage tough guys and their challenges to teachers and school authorities get them expelled. The police become their enemies and the result is often jail.

But the warrior fire does not stop burning. Those who get ignored, expelled, jailed, or left out of structured and supervised activities such as athletics form their own warrior cliques. We know them as Homeboys, Skinheads, Vice Lords, and Black Stone Rangers. Hungry to express their warrior prowess, they mark their territories, adopt their own uniforms and colors and create their own battlefields. Their rules, like the headhunters of Borneo, and the dueling fraternities of Europe, often involve killing and being killed.

This is not a new problem. Back in 1968, when Jim Brown, the famous running back of the Cleveland Browns football team, began working with youth gangs such as the Cripps and Bloods in Los Angeles County, 771 young men had already been killed in the ongoing territorial blood feuds that year, far more than the number of Americans killed in Desert Storm, the 1991 war in Iraq.

Schools play a major but largely unrecognized role in creating the criminal subculture. Schoolteachers and administrators who are unable to deal with young warriors and who in various ways separate them from the mainstream are unwittingly contributing new recruits for street gangs.

Providing more comprehensive sports and adventure programs with adult supervision that retain the dropouts and guide larger numbers of emerging warriors into constructive development and expression of their Animus powers is a better way to socialize young men than focusing so much attention on the chosen few outstanding athletes who make the team. Unfortunately, athletics in both high school and college have become powerful money-making entertainments for adults, and the result is that only a few of the most talented young men benefit. The vast majority never get to be football heroes or experience the powerful lessons that come from being part of a team.

Aggressive sports such as football, hockey, baseball, soccer, track and field, not to mention boxing and wrestling, provide legitimate forums for competitive encounters that are ideal outlets for the warrior drive. Adventure programs that involve mountain climbing, skiing, hunting, fishing, and working with horses also provide good tests of warrior skill and courage.

Supervised activities for emerging warriors also provide opportunities to learn about sportsmanship and what it means to be brave and manly. Notions of chivalry were a major element in the training of knights in mediaeval times. The proud warrior protected women and children, and rules of combat such as not shooting unarmed adversaries or not shooting enemies is in back were widespread, even in the "Wild West."

The tragic shooting spree at Columbine High School in Denver shows how twisted the warrior archetype can become when young men fall through the cracks. In a school with over two thousand students, relatively few young men "make the team." The fact that school athletes were primary targets is significant. The fact that one of the shooters had tried to enlist in the marines and had been turned down a few days before the mad rampage is also significant. The fact that they shot helpless, unarmed students, including young women, shows a lack of instruction about manliness, chivalry, and what it means to be a coward.

The eighteen-year-old Jason Hoffman, who took a rifle to his California high school and opened fire on fellow students only months after the Columbine tragedy, had also tried to join the Navy a few days before his rampage.

The warrior archetype flares at about the same age in every culture. All teenage men everywhere form clusters and find ways to "strut their stuff." In modern industrialized societies, movies, television, and videogames which dramatize the warrior archetype fan these flames. Without fathers, teachers, uncles, drill sergeants and other adult male instructors, they still form clusters; but the initiation rites and territorial wars of street gangs slip some critical cogs in the evolution of human ethics. They are both cruel and primitive. Drive-by shootings of innocent strangers become an initiation requirement in some youth gangs.

In the United States, the prison population now exceeds two million souls. The vast majority are young men. Poorly educated, underemployed, no longer able to vote, expelled, and in other ways pushed off the wagon of mainstream acculturation, they learn their ethics and new criminal occupations from other, usually older, inmates. In prisons and reform schools, kindness is seen as weakness. Hardness, ruthlessness, and the ability to inspire fear, the same values taught in military boot camps, are seen as admirable manly traits.

THE RECENT EMERGENCE OF THE FATHER ROLE

To fully understand the Anima archetype, it is important to push back the anthropological calendar to a time when Homo sapiens did not understand fundamental information about where babies come from. Early humans naturally concluded that babies came from women. It was logical for them to trace their lineage through women. In these earlier stages of human development, the concept of *father* did not exist, nor did our now common concept of *family*. It was a widespread practice for all the adult males of a tribe to live together in a common men's hut, separate from the females and children; this was typical. In fact, this pattern is still common in many of the remaining hunting and gathering societies. Female gods and the concept of the female creator flourished. The role of men in these societies was focused on the hunting of large animals and fighting tribal wars for survival and control of territory.

Malinowski[14] discovered that the Trobriand Island tribes knew nothing about the male role in creating babies. They believed women of the tribe became pregnant by passing close to holy places or being exposed to the foam in sea water.

Freud refers to very similar beliefs among tribes of the Arunta in central Australia, first reported in 1899 by Frazier and Gillen.[15] Since nine months pass between conception and birth, it is not too surprising that early humans may not

---

14. Malinowski, Bronislaw, *Argonauts of the Western Pacific; An Account of Native Enterprise & Adventure in the Archipelagoes of Melanesian New Guinea*, pref. By Sir James Frasier (New York: E. P Dutton & Co., Inc., 1961).

15. Freud, Sigmund, *Totem and Taboo*, op. cit.

have understood the relationship between sexual intercourse and babies. In these conditions, men felt no special kinship to newborn tribal members. To them, the children belonged to the women. In fact, it was relatively recent in human evolution that the concept of fathers and two-parent families emerged.

Some anthropologists believe that this knowledge was intertwined with the emergence of agriculture and the breeding and domestication of animals. Once humans understood the planting of seed, in its many forms, the male self image must have gone through some weighty changes. The revelation that men also had children and that children had fathers as well as mothers could not have been more profound. It probably contributed to the change from matrilineal to patrilineal tribes, from female to male gods, to the widespread worship of fertility deities, as well as to the formation of two-parent family structures. In *Totem and Taboo*, Freud noted that "with the introduction of father-deities a fatherless society gradually changed into one organized on a patriarchal basis."[16]

Recorded history is a relatively recent thing, in evolutionary terms. If the Bible is acknowledged as one of our oldest books, it is clear from the first chapter, in the story of Cain and Able, that both agriculture and pastoralism were already established. Cain raised sheep and goats. Able was a farmer. Perhaps the 10,000-year era of agriculture has allowed enough generations to pass to erase the traces of our foraging and hunting and gathering progenitors. On the other hand, one might argue that the reason so many fathers walk away from their children following unwanted pregnancies or divorces, spend so much time at work away from their families, demonstrate so little appetite for nurturing activities, and in general seem uninterested in child rearing may be due to the relatively recent emergence of the father role.

These subtle and poorly understood survival drives may lie at the root of dominance behavior exhibited by males of many species, including Homo sapiens. When a powerful male manages to out fight, out bluff, or outwit others in his struggle to become the alpha of a large pyramid, say, the United States government, perhaps his animal nature makes him look for other alphas of other pyramids so that he might continue his climb for increasing power and dominance.

---

16. Freud, Sigmund, *Totem and Taboo*, op. cit, page 149.

Chapter Five:
Corporate Hunting

Corporations have the same need for hunting as that of earlier tribal adaptations. They hunt for customers, for contracts, for sales. Their primary goal, like that of the gatherers, is to feed the tribe. In some corporate tribes such as Boeing or McDonald Douglas, teams of big game hunters work together to land contracts large enough to feed huge numbers of employees for years. In others, armies of field sales representatives must scour their territories daily, aggressively following every lead in order to provide their tribes with the sales required to grow and prosper.

Tremendous teamwork was required to successfully hunt whales in the waters off Alaska. Each tribe had to finely tune its skills and techniques, depending on its territory and the animals it hunted. So, too, must corporations develop and refine their hunting methods depending on their products, territories and customers.

Corporate hunters often travel long distances and work for hours and days to find and approach customers, and they feel the same flush of pride and success when their hunt is successful and they make the sale.

Weapons

Although there are clear parallels in the way corporate and more primitive hunters identify and stalk their quarry, the weapons have changed dramatically.

When corporate hunters leave for a hunting trip, they no longer carry spears, knives, and blow guns. They carry a briefcase. Their weapons have evolved into brochures, slide shows, and written proposals.

Hunting has become a matter of verbal persuasion, a mental rather than a physical challenge. Every corporation should ask itself, "How sharp are our weapons?" The verbal, graphic and electronic weapons of the corporate hunter must impress and persuade.

A consultant opens his computer, pushes a button, and a beautiful Powerpoint slide show unfolds. This silver, book-sized computer magically delivers a highly persuasive sales pitch. When the time arrives to open one's briefcase and pull out one's weapons, they must be devastating.

Hunting with old bait or with weapons that have lost their edge is difficult and frustrating.

Ron Martin is a big game hunter. He sells folding cartons to food companies and department stores. If he can get a contract to provide a printed cereal package for a Post or General Mills, or a cardboard wrapper for a beer or soft drink company, he can keep his company's plant operating for months or even years. His efforts generate millions in revenue for his company..

Every August, Ron rents a 30-foot long recreation vehicle, fills its coolers with beer and drives it and six purchasing agents from his major customers to a fishing camp in Canada. They play cards, drink beer, tell bad jokes, belch, fart and laugh till their sides ache. In Canada they fish for pike and walleye during the day and play liar's dice in the evenings. They almost never discuss business or packaging. The relationships Ron has so skillfully cultivated go far beyond the typical customer contact. All this time, he is hunting them.

As unfair as it may seem to female sales agents, Ron's formula for success relies heavily on male bonding.

In many corporations, all the current and potential customers in a given region or territory are well known and in order to get a new customers, one has to dislodge a competitor. Using the customer herd analogy, there are few or no stray cows available, and in order for a corporate tribe to increase its herd, cows must be taken away from a competitor. The skillful corporate hunter must be patient and persistent, waiting for moments of vulnerability such as after his enemy has submitted a large bill, when a competitor's sales representative has been transferred to a new territory, or when the person doing the buying is new.

When old or existing relationships are disrupted, the opportunity for establishing new ones open up.

Buffalo Robes

When the Blackfoot and Mandan Indians of the central plains hunted buffalo, they would drape buffalo robes over themselves and their horses. This allowed them to get close enough to the herds to be effective with their lances and arrows. They looked and smelled like buffalos.

Similar tactics were used to hunt antelope. Certain hunters would tie on antelope hides, then dance and flop around on the ground to attract the antelopes' attention. The skilled antelope dancer understood the curious nature of antelopes and could bring the animals close enough so that the hunt could succeed.

A similar principle operates in corporate hunting. A skilled corporate hunter knows that he must dress, smell, and talk just like his quarry. A plaid jacket, a spot of gravy on the tie, a bad haircut, too much cologne or not enough deodorant and the sale can be lost. In some situations, a suit, a tie and a white shirt will be inappropriate. In others, that is the only costume that will work. The right clothes, language, and smell allows the hunter to get close to his customers and this closeness is essential to put them at ease so that the process of communicating and building trust can begin.

Too many hunters get it right during a sales pitch, then blow it at the end by relaxing and letting slip some word or gesture — like lighting a cigarette — that alienates his client. The camouflage has to be kept in place until the hunt is over.

Corporate hunting involves a rich variety of activities, but most include traveling away from the corporate headquarters. The distances traveled to acquire food also distinguished hunters from gatherers in primitive tribes. Hunters traveled further and were first to penetrate the hunting grounds of competing tribes.

The distinction between hunting and gathering, Animus and Anima, in corporate employment can be seen in the way employees are hired. In the typical employment function ads are placed in the local newspaper and the gatherers remain within the corporate compound while they screen and interview applicants.

Executive search, by contrast, is a hunting function. It is even referred to as "headhunting." Here the quarry is identified, stalked, and must be lured in, or "sold" on the idea of changing companies. Executive recruiters are often outside experts, hired guns, who travel extensively. They must travel out into the fields where the game is located.

Where accounts receivable is clearly a gathering function, securing a new line of credit is a hunting activity. Here, as in executive recruiting, the hunter travels out into some distant territory, away from the tribal compound, to seek the quarry. In this case, the quarry is a bank and the hunter must perform a kind of verbal ritual, a presentation designed to persuade. If the business plan makes sense, and appears to be prudent, the hunter may succeed in getting the credit his corporation needs.

CORPORATE HUNTERS

Corporations are well aware of the importance of selecting and developing an effective sales force. Many corporations, particularly insurance companies, have spent enormous amounts trying to figure out how to select individuals who are likely to succeed. The investment in orientation and training, coupled with the huge failure rate, represent a major drain on the budget.

Skilled corporate hunters come in a variety of shapes, sizes, and personalities; and the hunter who succeeds in selling real estate or insurance may not succeed selling computers or consulting contracts.

The hunter must fit the tribe and the product. In spite of numerous attempts to develop tests and interview methods, the single best way to pick winners is still a strong record of past sales of similar products to similar customers.

However, recognizing the archetypal role of tribal hunter puts a unique spin on selection criterion. Of course, the true hunter loves the hunt. He or she must enjoy travel, searching for prospective customers, the competition, and the thrill of closing the sale. The same patience and persistence required for fishing, and the same knowledge of baits, lures, and how to locate the quarry, are essential for corporate hunting. These methods and techniques change with each product and must be learned from those with experience.

Chapter Five: Corporate Hunting

In the corporate tribal mutation, where capturing mind share and relationship building are essential to successful selling, interpersonal sensitivity and the ability to listen well may be more important than pure persuasiveness. On the other hand, if the task is selling vegetable slicers at the state fair, sensitivity may be a disadvantage. As in primitive hunting, there is no need to build a relationship.

Hunters must be skillful in their use of weapons. They know when to pull out the brochure, how to quickly and accurately calculate prices and discounts, how to operate the laptop and slide projector, and how to conduct flawless product demonstrations. (Nothing kills a sale like an electrical problem with the slide show.)

They enjoy competition, particularly winning. Those with team experience make the best pack hunters. Individual hunters are more likely to be tennis players, runners, golfers or wrestlers.

They dress well and look sharp. They project confidence. Like knights in shining armor and war chiefs with magnificent displays of feathers, their appearance shows a flair for display and style.

They prefer decisive action, activity, and *doing* to analysis, contemplation, and intellectual discussion. They want to participate rather than spectate. They run, play sports, and engage in competitive, strenuous physical activity rather than leading sedentary lives.

Good sales reps are sociable. They like meeting people and usually have a good sense of humor. They know how to get close to their customers.

During the interview, the candidate for a sales position is attempting to sell himself or herself. The customer is likely to respond the same way the interviewer does; so if the interviewer is sold, the customer is likely to be sold as well.

How to Develop Corporate Hunters

Making corporate sales representatives aware of their archetypal tribal roles can enhance their effectiveness just as it does with tribal gatherers. There is already a dim awareness. Many corporations use phrases such as "bring home the bacon" and "hunting for new accounts" to describe sales activities. The analogy is far more obvious than with corporate gathering.

There is still no substitute for pairing up a new hunter with an experienced one. They need to watch each other. Most corporations are well aware of the need for providing hands on coaching and active training in product knowledge, presentation skills, and closing techniques. These essential elements of selling must be learned, but the basic hunter attitude and temperament may well be at least partially genetic.

Selling is a kind of ritual. The customer is fully aware of the salesperson's motives and intentions. Every adult has participated in this ritual a thousand times, so the sales person must say and do the right things in the right order to establish a relationship. Ultimately, customers allow themselves to be sold. Conducting this ritual with interpersonal skill, humor, and sensitivity is the key to success.

Where establishing and building relationships requires interpersonal skill and sensitivity, closing the sale often requires a streak of ruthlessness. Show too much sympathy when a customer hesitates or objects to something, and the sale is lost. In hunting and combat, delivering the death blow requires timing, resolve and a suspension of sympathy. The hunter must give his primary sympathy to feeding his tribe.

The Corporate War Dance

Once or twice each year, corporations call all the hunters in from their territories. They are given new weapons (brochures, models, and discount programs). They discuss new products. They plan new sales campaigns and discuss the activities of their enemies. The successful hunters make presentations about how they stalked their prey and brought down the big buffalos. They drink fire water and are filled with enthusiasm by inspiring speakers. Then they are sent back into their territories, eager to continue their battle.

Most corporations are completely unaware that their annual sales meeting is an ancient tribal ritual.

Marketing as Scouting

In hunting and gathering tribes, certain hunters specialized in moving out in front of their tribes, exploring new territories, locating game, tracking the movements of enemy hunters, and bringing information back to the tribe that helped them plan their movements and migrations. They gathered intelligence.

They helped plan hunting campaigns and raids on enemy camps. They advised on new weapons and hunting methods and became experts on camouflage, traps and snares.

This function still exists in modern corporations. *Marketing* has evolved into a variety of complex and sophisticated techniques and methods, but it still fulfills an ancient and critical function, one that works closely with the hunters and gatherers and contributes dramatically to the growth and survival of the tribe.

In *Marketing Warfare*[17], Al Ries and Jack Trout show how modern marketing strategies make use of ancient principles of warfare to outflank competitors and capture market share. They describe defensive warfare principles for market leaders, offensive warfare for the No. 2 or No. 3 company in a field, and guerrilla warfare for all the others. Their descriptions of the cola, beer, burger, and computer wars leave little doubt that many ancient principles of territorial warfare still apply.

---

17. Ries, Al and Trout, Jack, *Marketing Warfare* (New York: McGraw-Hill, Inc. 1986).

CHAPTER SIX:
CORPORATE WARFARE

Corporate presidents and vice presidents of sales and marketing, those who stay abreast of the big picture, are well aware that the competition for growth and survival of their companies is a kind of warfare. Within a given market, for example in the selling of automobiles, a zero sum game is still a fact of corporate life. This market has a fixed limit and increases in market share can only come at the expense of direct competitors.

Many employees are only partially aware that their raises, bonuses, ability to send their children to college or buy a new car, even their jobs are largely dependant on how well their corporate tribe conducts warfare against key competitors.

Employees tend to focus their frustrations and resentments on obvious targets, their own management. Many would not be able to name their major competitors; but when these competitors capture market share through better products or services, or more effective advertising, they can force layoffs and downsizing. And if the trend is not reversed, a losing company can become an easy target for acquisition.

Success in corporate warfare means growth. Failure results first in shrinkage, and then acquisition or bankruptcy.

It is difficult to apply some of the concepts in Sun Tzu's 2500-year-old book *The Art of War*[18] to corporate warfare. There are clear and obvious differences in the way armies of the agricultural Chinese conducted battle and the way corporations do it. Carl von Clausewitz was also writing about standing armies of the agricultural era in his famous book, *On War*.[19] Nonetheless, many basic principles do still apply; for example, the principle that larger armies defeat smaller ones. Large corporations with bigger sales forces and advertising budgets can usually protect their markets and take market share from smaller companies. Both Sun Tzu and von Clausewitz warned generals about attacking enemies that had superior forces. Wise generals choose their battles carefully, selecting weaker, smaller opponents, or concentrating their forces on an opponent's weakest link.

One company that had studied Sun Tzu and understood how to apply the principle of superior force was in the business of developing film. Their target customers were drugstores, convenience stores, and shopping centers where people could drop of their exposed rolls of film for developing and pick them up a day later.

They knew every film-developing outlet in their assigned territory, those they serviced as well as those serviced by their competitors. They were not the largest film developer in their territory, so when they formed their marketing and sales plan they targeted a smaller competitor and declared a secret war to defeat him.

First, they identified all of their competitor's accounts. Second, they focused on ten key accounts, for example a Target store in Cedar Rapids, that represented an anchor customer. They determined that if they could take away the anchor customer in a given territory, it would not be profitable for their competitor to attempt to service smaller customers in the same area; so that a number of these smaller accounts would also become available.

The third thing they did was form ten commando teams, each assigned to one of the key accounts. Each commando team consisted of a sales representative, a customer service representative, and a factory representative. Each team was given the task of forming a strategy for capturing their assigned account within the coming year.

When the teams presented their strategies, no two were alike. One focused on hiring the competitor's sales representative who called on the key account. Another focused on researching the store manager's background,

---

18. Sun Tzu *The Art of War*, Trans. Tomas Cleary (New York: Shambhala Publications, Inc., 1991).
19. von Clausewitz, Carl, *On War* (London: the Penguin Classics; Viking Press; 1982).

Chapter Six: Corporate Warfare

hobbies, and interests and then using this information to establish a relationship. A third relied on persistence. The sales rep would call on the store once a week for 52 weeks, if necessary. There were discount packages and programs for new in-store signage and special promotions.

As the year unfolded, some of the target accounts began to tumble. With each conquest, big announcements and accolades were published in the company newsletter. The competitor, unaware that it was the target of a coordinated strategy, suffered serious losses in its customer base and sales volume. The commando teams grew more bold and confident. Bonuses increased for everyone.

Understanding ancient principles of tribal warfare, and applying them wisely, can make a huge difference in the competitive success of a modern corporation.

Territory

In hunting-gathering tribes, territory meant hunting grounds and preferred foraging lands. In the agricultural era, territory was cropland. In both cases controlling a territory meant food and survival. Defending one's territory from exploitation by others was and is necessary, for humans just as it is for other higher carnivores. This is how hunting and war became so intimately linked. The skills required for success were similar. Both required weapons. Only the quarry changed.

> Anthony Willoughby, founder of *I Will Not Complain, Inc.*, a company that provides team-building courses for corporations in China and Japan, has been sitting down with New Guinea tribal chiefs to collect drawings of their tribal territories. The drawings always include the main tribal compound, the hunting territory, garden plots, sacred places such as grave yards, important rivers or fishing regions, and major roads or trails.
>
> Willoughby also collects hand-drawn maps of tribal territory from corporate employees and chief executives, then guides them through a tribal analysis of such basic questions as, "Where does your food come from? How much will you need to sustain your growth plans for next year? Who is threatening your hunting grounds? Where is your frontier?" and "Where is your home territory?"
>
> One of the more consistent themes that emerges in Willoughby's meetings is the need and desire to expand into new territories in order to support tribal/corporate growth.

As of November 2000, Willoughby had collected 350 hand drawn maps of corporate territories. He is amazed by their similarity. One executive asked him if they had been drawn by the same individual. He believes he is tapping into instinctive fears and concerns regarding tribal survival. He believes that corporate employees already understand the fundamentals of tribal territory at some instinctual gut level. They deal with it, with different labels, every day.

Willoughby's analysis of the 350 maps of corporate territory has yielded four reoccurring themes. First, employees feel their food source territories are under threat. None feels completely secure. Second, to survive and grow, the tribe needs to expand into new territories. Third, tribal leaders are isolated or are unable to mobilize and lead the needed migration. Fourth, internal issues need to be resolved before the migration can begin.

Every corporate tribe hunts within territories and its ability to command or dominate a given territory is measured by its market share.

Most mature corporations have a home territory where they own, dominate or control a market. Their warfare is essentially defensive in nature. In these areas they assign more hunter/sales representatives, who work smaller patches of territory. They out-man and outspend competitors for advertising and promotions, and out-discount those who attempt to invade or get a foothold. The basic principle — that defending a territory is more often successful than attacking and dislodging an enemy who is already dug in — clearly applies to corporate warfare.

The "cola wars" present many good examples. Pepsi ran a training seminar for some of its most aggressive, highly creative sales representatives and put them into what they called their "frontier" territories.

These were territories like Atlanta, where Coca Cola had the major share of the market. Pepsi tried to steal bits of market share by surprising or outflanking their arch enemy. If they could sign a big name entertainer, such as Cheryl Crow or Willie Nelson, to sponsor Pepsi at the state fair, they were seen as great heroes. These sales representatives were seen as hit and run guerilla fighters.

In their home territories, Pepsi was more entrenched and their strategies were essentially defensive. Here the sales representatives tended mature working relationships with large long time customers. These hunters were older men and women who had worked their way into these favored position by a history of strong performance. When an employee was promoted to one of these positions, he or she took over a "book" of major customers that guaranteed a substantial commission. Losing one of these customers, McDonald's, for example, was a cardinal sin.

Chapter Six: Corporate Warfare

Pepsi was quick to reward representatives who could gain market share and just as quick to fire those who could not compete with a very able adversary. In the cola wars, the casualty rate was shocking.

In order for a corporation to invade a new patch of territory, it must first secure a beachhead. It does this with its marines, known in corporations as National Accounts Representatives. These are often the corporate tribe's sharpest, best trained, most persuasive hunters. Their objective is to secure a few anchor accounts, hopefully big ones.

Once a beachhead is established, the army of sales reps can begin to move in. A sales office can be opened with the sales support and customer service staff needed to sustain this corporate outpost.

As the customer base and market share grows, more sales reps are added. Eventually a castle, fort, factory is built and this reduces shipping costs and further cements power and control over a patch of territory.

In the competition among corporate tribes, territory is often something other than a patch of ground. An automobile represents a kind of territory. Suppliers fight with all their resources to see who will supply brakes, dashboards, engines, frames, drive trains, gears, exhaust systems, air bags and seats. Every part and piece of an automobile becomes a theater for a bloodless war where the winners get huge contracts that allow their tribes to grow while the losers must downsize.

The battle strategies and maneuvers in these corporate wars are top secret, hashed out behind closed doors; but a rare glimpse was possible during a lawsuit between Litton and Honeywell in a fight to dominate the navigation-gear market in jetliners. It was reported by William M. Carley in the *Wall Street Journal* on September 20, 1996.[20]

The battle to see who would supply "ring-laser gyroscopes" for various jetliners, including Boeing's 757 narrow bodies, and 767 widebodies, Airbus Industrie's A-320, and McDonnell Douglas's MD-90, lasted for years and eventually involved KLM, Lufthansa, Aerospatiale, and Alitalia.

> Honeywell's motivation [a Boeing memo states], was to establish themselves firmly as Boeing's IRS (inertial-reference system) supplier and to prohibit Litton from entering the Boeing market.

---

20. Carley, William M., *Air War, How Honeywell Beat Litton to Dominate Navigation-Gear Field* (New York: The Wall Street Journal, September 20, 1996).

> Honeywell attacked at a key Litton customer, Airbus Industries, in what became the climactic battle....Honeywell became sole supplier of laser gyros on the small Airbus A-320 partly by paying Airbus $1 million in lieu of a price cut.

...in 1991, Litton made a secret agreement with Aerospatiale, the Airbus consortium member that builds Airbus cockpits and has a major say on instruments. Litton would pay the French company $3 million annually for engineering costs and a "preferred position," meaning Litton expected to get its gyros on 65% or more of A-330s, A-340s and the A-321, a new small jet.

But Honeywell got wind of the strategy — a Litton "under the table deal" with Aerospatiale, one Honeywell memo called it — and Honeywell set out to undermine it by going directly to an Airbus customer, Alitalia.

> ...safety authorities were pressing Alitalia to install windshear detectors on its older jets, and Honeywell, a producer of windshear detectors as a result of its Sperry acquisition, offered the instruments for free plus other price breaks that Honeywell valued at $13 million — if Alitalia would buy Honeywell's gyro.

Litton lost. The Honeywell concessions to Alitalia were "so overwhelming that we couldn't afford to match them," Litton's Mr. Sprink testified. From the early 1980s through 1993, according to a Litton count of sales to the big three aircraft producers, Honeywell sold 11,944 ring-laser gyros and Litton 1,099.

In this corporate battle, the territory was the cockpit of jetliners and Honeywell was the winner. It had more ammunition, already controlled most of the territory, and was able to defend its position effectively. It was not a bloody war, but it was clearly a ruthless one.

At the same time, Airbus and Boeing-McDonnell Douglas have been competing to sell jets to airlines around the world. At this level, national and regional loyalties weigh in heavily; the stakes are so high that direct economic efficiencies may be minor factors in the final equation. We will discuss divided loyalties in greater detail, below.

For the modern food-producing corporation, territory is often grocery store shelf space where the preferred eye level positions become the prize and sales reps from competing food companies tussle to expand display areas. Competitors typically offer special discounts or free advertising to induce stores to take more of their products.

Chapter Six: Corporate Warfare

Territory can also be key pages for advertising in a major magazine and 30-second TV commercials during the Super Bowl. Only the big boys with lots of financial resources can afford to lob these advertising A-bombs. Corporate warfare involves competition to control markets which are more abstract and diverse kinds of territory than land; but the battles, though bloodless, are none the less intense and the rewards can involve billions of dollars.

Another such battle involved Charlie Ergen, Chairman of EchoStar, and the notorious Rupert Murdoch. These industry Samurai fought over rapidly growing satellite-TV market estimated at over $10 billion in revenues in the US in 2002, serving 20% of pay-TV customers. The prize was Hughes Electronics and its Direct TV operation. Andy Pasztor and John Lippman reported the battle in *The Wall Street Journal*.[21]

> When satellite-television upstart EchoStar Communications Corp. emerged as the surprise winner in the bidding for Hughes Electronics Corp. last year, Rupert Murdoch left a message on the home phone of EchoStar Chairman Charlie Ergen graciously conceding defeat.
>
> But a day later, top lieutenants at Mr. Murdoch's News Corp. began secretly plotting to undermine the multibillion-dollar deal.
>
> Knowing that the deal would give EchoStar a near monopoly, 90% of the satellite-television market in the US, and that this would be the Achilles heel when seeking the approval of federal regulators, Murdoch's top strategists launched an all out word-of-mouth campaign aimed at scuttling the deal. They hired former New York state attorney general Robert Abrams, a seasoned political wizard, to build opposition among state and local government agencies, and made sited presentations to broadcasters and consumer groups. Murdoch even spoke to a convention of religious broadcasters, who worried that Ergen and EchoStar would drop their programs if the merger went through. It worked. Opposition to the deal spread and federal regulators in Washington blocked the acquisition. Murdoch's strategy involved more than revenge. He wanted to acquire Direct TV for his own company.

Great battles like these rage daily among large corporations. The winners make fortunes. The losers regroup and go on to the next battle. The competition requires creativity, resources, and intelligent strategy, but no blood is shed.

---

21. Pasztor, Andy and Robert Lippman, *Crossed Signals — How a Dream Deal in Satellite TV Ran into Static* (New York: The Wall Street Journal, October 9, 2002) page 1.

MISSILES AND BOMBS

In bloody war, the invasion of a new patch of territory was usually preceded by a hail of missiles and bombs. In the bloodless wars of corporations, these have evolved into mass mailings and TV advertising. Mass mail campaigns are like a hail of arrows. Thousands are sent into the target market, but only a few find their mark. To capture the mind share of millions, one needs a national television ad campaign on Super Bowl Sunday, the equivalent of an atomic bomb.

As experienced warriors know, no amount of missiles and bombs can, by themselves, secure a new patch of territory. Once again, the principle holds true for corporations. An advertising barrage can raise awareness and create a demand, but sales reps must follow to make human contact, look the new customer in the eye and press the flesh.

The maddening telephone calls one receives at dinnertime are the work of beaters. Huge banks of telephone solicitors, assisted by automatic dialing computers, make thousands of telephone calls daily — and when they find someone who will listen to their pitch, they point. Like hunting dogs, they direct the hunters to their targets.

PAINTBALL BATTLES

With so much attention focused on soft internal issues such as leaderless groups, collaborative problem solving, product quality, team building and communications effectiveness, it is easy to lose the aggressive and competitive edge needed to grow market share. One method for reviving the warrior fire in the sales group and getting it focused on its competition is the paint ball exercise.

> While discussing the latest sales and marketing campaign at the annual sales meeting, several men dressed in camouflage with painted faces and automatic weapons suddenly burst into the room. They knock over the flip charts, grab the confidential marketing plan, fire warning bursts, then quickly run out of the room.
>
> This wakes everyone up and sets the stage for a paintball exercise.
>
> The sales force is given the task of getting the marketing plan back. They must gather as much information about their enemy as possible. They must put together a battle plan. They are issued single shot weapons, protective clothing, face masks and goggles. They are given target practice and

Chapter Six: Corporate Warfare

limited ammunition. They are given battlefield rules. They go after the enemy and try to recapture their highly valuable and confidential marketing plans.

Paintball exercises are fun and exciting. The true warriors quickly emerge as well as those who are too timid, passive, or cautious to be effective. The VP of Sales learns a lot about his people and they learn a lot about their boss. The team's approach to planning is observed for later discussion. Their communications and skill at executing their plan is observed. Their effectiveness as a team is discussed.

And for months afterward, war stories abound during coffee breaks.

Paintball exercises would only be fun and games were it not for the discussions which follows. The company's real enemies (competitors) are named and discussed at length. The real sales and marketing plans are reviewed. The aggressive and competitive juices aroused during the paintball battle are focused on real competition for market share. Weapons (sales tools and materials) are examined. Ammunition (cash and other resources) is considered.

The team's actual performance is also discussed, especially its ability to adapt and maintain communications and teamwork under fire. How effective was their battle plan? Who sacrificed for the team? What might they have done to sustain fewer casualties? How can the lessons of the exercise be applied to their real situation?

In the planning of paintball exercises it is important to provide non-combat roles for those who are uncomfortable with the notion of armed competition. They can serve as ammo bearers or battlefield judges.

It is also important that a team is not divided and forced to fight each other. This could encourage internal competition and destroy team effort. It is best that the entire team focus on a common enemy. In our approach, one trained enemy with an automatic weapon is assigned for every five company team members with single shot weapons. Paintball exercises provide a vehicle for redirecting the attention of those who are focused on internal issues, to external issues such as the marketplace, customers and key competitors.

It arouses warrior emotions and enhances the aggressiveness of sales and marketing professionals.

As is the case with many team exercises, paintball games usually bring out real issues in dysfunctional teams.

One company had a particularly dysfunctional sales team. The boss was a cranky, angry fellow who had been passed over for the CEO position and been made VP of sales and marketing instead He had not won the allegiance of his new team and, in truth, had done little to earn it.

His top producing sales manager appeared to be actively undermining his new boss. He too had been passed over for VP Sales and when the new boss arrived, he was not hesitant to point out the man's shortcomings.

On a retreat aimed to enhance the teamwork, the signs of dysfunction were clear from the very beginning. Every time the boss spoke, his sales manager disagreed with him and the team clearly took the sales manager's side. The planning session was chaotic, but eventually two teams were formed, neither of which included the new boss. When the teams divided to surround the enemy position, the boss followed along behind one of them.

The greatly outnumbered enemy raiders, trained veterans of many paintball battles, were delighted to see the team divide. It was clearly to their advantage to face two smaller forces. And when they noted that one of the participants was wandering on his own, they quickly surrounded him and took him out. The boss was the first casualty.

The dysfunctional elements of the teams' performance were discussed at length during the debriefing session and some important lessons surfaced. But they did not save the new boss. Within three months, he was asked to leave the company. The disloyal sales manager was promoted to replace him. It was a good decision.

In those paintball battles where the boss led the troops and demonstrated courage and adaptability under pressure, the team's allegiance clearly increased.

In paintball battles, when entire departments are involved, some of the women may be among the most eager and effective fighters, although others, both men and women, may be either disinterested or actively opposed to the whole idea of playing at war. One woman who declined to be a warrior in a pending paintball battle agreed to be an ammo bearer instead, and as her team moved forward through the trees she stayed in the rear with a bag full of tubes filled with paint balls.

Her team ran directly into the jaws of an enemy ambush and within two minutes the entire front line was decimated. What happened next was unforgettable. She bypassed the single shot weapons of her fallen comrades and went instead to one of the fallen enemy. She took his automatic weapon, then charged like a banshee into the enemy nest, spraying paintballs in a circle around her like Rambo. She shot four of them and more or less turned the tide.

Afterward, she seemed almost embarrassed by the praise of her comrades; her hands were still trembling. It was like something in her leaped out, her she-bear, and meeting this powerful internal force had shocked her.

Everyone who worked with her also learned something. She was no longer just the kind, cooperative colleague they had known. There was fierceness in her, and great courage.

A curious phenomenon occurs in these exercises. In large mixed groups, the casualty rate among men is consistently two or three times greater than that of women. Men typically rush to the front, try to be heroic, or perhaps protective, and get shot. At times, this disproportionate casualty rate seems like an echo from the tribal warfare of our past. In terms of species or gene pool survival, men are more expendable than child-bearing woman.

The fact that athletic games have been around for centuries while wars raged indicate that athletic competition may not be enough to reduce the appetite and tendency for war. Of course, many have made the case that war is a kind of territorial game for powerful men. The soldiers are the pawns, the cannon fodder. It is always a bit shocking to learn that generals have treated one another with courtesy and restraint during formal surrenders, while thousands of bodies were still cooling on the field of battle.

On the other hand, television has so amplified the popularity of professional sports that millions of armchair warriors get a healthy weekly dose. Owners of these teams can make huge fortunes, more than the spoils of earlier wars. We should not underestimate the ability of professional sports to supplant and replace the lust for war.

Chapter Seven:
The Wizard Archetype

Tribes in Mexico call them *brujos*. In parts of Africa, they are known as fetishers. In Caribbean tribes they are known as witch doctors and native Americans referred to them as medicine men. They are persons who are seen as having some kind of special knowledge about the world. They are healers, seers, sorcerers, explainers of things like thunder, comets, disease, death, the afterlife, spirits, love, and the gods. They are both feared and revered.

In the late 1800s, Herbert Spenser compiled hundreds of detailed accounts of shamans in various parts of the world and explained some possible scenarios of how they came to be seen as having power over evil spirits. Among the Colombian Indians, for example, the medicine-man "proceeds to force the evil spirit from the sick man by pressing both clenched fists with all his might in the pit of his stomach". Of the inspired Fijian priest it is said, "All his words and actions are considered as no longer his own, but those of the deity who has entered into him....While giving the answer, the priest's eyes stand out and roll as in a frenzy; his voice is unnatural, his face pale, his lips livid, his breathing depressed, and his entire appearance like that of a furious madman."

Among Californian tribes, the doctor "squats down opposite the patient and barks at him after the manner of an enraged cur, for hours". In Sumatra, a shaman tried to expel the evil spirit that causes insanity by putting the insane person into a hut, which they set fire to, leaving him to escape as best he can. [22] Although these remedies seem absurd to modern sensibilities, the practice of exorcism, still practiced in some religions, springs from the same idea that illness and crazy behavior is caused by evil spirits.

Like hunters and gatherers, the tribal role of wizard is archetypal. It exists in all human clusters. But unlike hunters and gatherers of earlier tribal adaptations, the wizard role was never gender specific. A tribal wizard can be either a man or a woman.

In parts of Africa, certain wizards established such impressive reputations that they traveled from tribe to tribe to handle problems too serious for the local tribal wizards. Perhaps these were the first consultants.

When agriculture emerged and the first stable villages were founded and food surpluses occurred, religions became organized and institutionalized. The first permanent houses of worship emerged and the world became populated with shrines, temples, cathedrals, and houses of ceremony and worship. The organized religions of the agricultural era became more powerful. Tribal wizards evolved into priests, priestesses, and court wise men and women. They were seen as being able to influence rain and conducted elaborate fertility rites to insure successful harvests. As spokespeople for gods, they had great perceived power. They threw bones, read tea leaves, prayed to various gods, conducted healing ceremonies, interpreted dreams, and consulted the stars in orders to solve pressing problems and predict future events. They prepared medications, studied metals, chemicals, and the heavens; they conducted ceremonies, and created schools, societies, and priesthoods to pass along their accumulating knowledge.

In many societies, the priests and religious leaders became more powerful than the kings and queens they served. In ancient Egypt, several of the pharaohs were so encumbered by ceremonies and activities prescribed by priests that they were largely immobilized, leaving the priests to run things. On many occasions, a wizard succeeded to become chief.

The natives of Pau Pau, New Guinea live in constant fear of sorcery. When people become sick or die, or when violent storms rock their forest homelands, they suspect that someone among them has cast an evil spell. Great waves of paranoia sweep over them until the witch or demon is discovered and either

---

22.Spencer, Herbert *The Principles of Sociology Vol.1-1* (New York, D. Appleton and Company, 1897)PP240-241.

killed, banished or appeased. They hear the voices of spirits in bird calls, thunder, and rushing forest streams.

The archetypal shaman, wizard, priest, with the perceived power to heal or curse others and the ability to talk with and interpret God's thoughts and feelings, is a part of every human's life experience..

As the organized religions of the agricultural era grew and became more powerful, and church buildings and temples emerged all over the earth, human tribes evolved into religious congregations. Much of the clustering of human groups occurred in churches and temples, under the leadership of priests, monks, and prophets.

As the creators of tribal ceremonies, interpreters of the universe, and spokesmen for the gods, priests and religious wizards still control the thinking of billions, for better or worse. Much of the worlds great art, music, literature and architecture emerged from world views generated by religious wizards. Much of the kindness, charity and love human beings show one another is rooted in the teachings of their particular religions. Of course we tend to refer to someone else's religion as their mythology and would feel insulted if our own cherished beliefs were called myths.

But together with all the good things religious mythologies promulgate, there have also been some horrendous things. The inquisitions, the crusades, millions of humans living with the fear of hell, and hundreds of bloody wars waged against sinners, infidels, gentiles, atheists, heretics, Muslims, Hindus, Catholics and Protestants. What went wrong in the religious interpretations of Mayan priests that resulted in human sacrifice, ripping out the heart of unfortunate victims and drinking the blood of their enemies. What powerful shaman or priest first persuaded them that these horrible ceremonies would please their gods or assure a good harvest.

The perceived power of the Pope, the majesty of the Catholic Church, its famous struggles for dominance with various secular governments and other religions, and its ability to prescribe behavior for so many millions show that the influence of the wizard archetype is real and enduring. And whether the wizard is adorned in a robe with a hood, like Merlin, a black cone shaped hat like a Halloween witch, the elaborate feathered head dress of an Aztec priest, or the red satin cloak and crown of a Catholic cardinal, he or she is playing out the same ancient archetypal role.

Wizards in Mythology and Real Life

In the biblical story, Joseph gained great power by interpreting Pharaoh's dreams. Merlin seemed to empower, guard and protect King Arthur. This same basic duo, the wizard and the king, is a common theme in all tribal mythology. Kings and presidents still have their technical advisors and experts who serve as their wizards. And the tribes with the best wizards usually win. When Moses threw down his staff, it transformed into a snake. But the Pharaoh's court wizards also knew the snake trick. They also transformed their rods into snakes. Then Moses demonstrated his superiority: his snake devoured the others.

Wizards are intellectuals. They are more interested in ideas than actions, decisions, and target dates. Some are a bit eccentric, awkward in social situations. Unlike warriors who love to strut and wear plumes, shiny armor, and chests full of medals, wizards tend to be a more tweedy, a bit rumpled, with chalk on their sleeves.

Where young developing warriors love the action and competition of sports, developing wizards show a natural interest in intellectual pursuits such as reading, chess, and scientific analysis and research. Known as bookworms, nerds, or geeks in high school, they often get good grades. They are inventive and fascinated by science and technology.

Dens of Wizards

One of the ceremonies wizards perform in all tribes is the rite of passage. In modern times, these rites include commencement, bar mitzvahs and other ceremonies. Our modern universities are dens of wizards. The robes that professors wear at graduation are descended from early universities and societies for science; perhaps they even resemble druid robes like those depicted in Camelot and Harry Potter.

Diplomas are handed out by robed men and women who are PhD researchers, professors, and authors — men and women who are acknowledged as authorities by other wizards in their particular fields of science. They are men and women of knowledge. As deans and college professors, they have dedicated their lives to preparing the next generation of corporate tribesmen and women, as well as to the identification, nurturing, and development of the next generation of wizards.

Corporate Wizards

The archetypal wizard role is alive and well in modern corporations. They are relatively easy to identify because they have letters after their names such a CPA, PhD, and MSE. Every field of study or endeavor which requires mastery of a body of knowledge has its wizards. But corporate tribes, by their nature, rely heavily on five or six basic kinds of wizards. We all know them well. They are *financial wizards, legal wizards, research scientists, engineering wizards, information technology wizards and headshrinkers*. They are referred to as "staff" versus "line" functions. Without their professional knowledge and skills, no large corporation could function.

When the Burlington Northern railroad spun off El Paso Natural Gas Company, creating two separate companies, each with its own stock, the stockholders must have been delighted. The stock of both companies went up. Some financial wizard who had a vision and understood the mind set of Wall Street and investors created more millions for Burlington Northern stockholders in this one brilliant maneuver than all the hard work and steady effort thousands of employees could have achieved in years.

The Pfizer scientists who created Viagra, and the researchers at G.D. Searle who perfected the first birth control pill, created billions in profits for their tribes. Their discoveries also changed the world.

Werner Von Braun and other German rocket wizards might have been executed for developing the V-2 rockets that fell on Great Britain killing innocent civilians and terrorizing the population. Instead they were protected, and then nurtured and encouraged because their knowledge of ballistic missiles held the promise of a military advantage. They too changed the world.

No one knows how many thousands of hours the ancient alchemists spent trying to turn lead into gold. Our modern investment bankers do it every day. The merger and acquisition wizards at Smith Barney and Goldman Sachs create billions of dollars on a regular basis when they take corporations public.

The power of many tribal wizards relies on the beliefs and faith of people they serve. They put on frightening masks, shake their rattles and pray to their tribal gods to cure a sick member of their tribe. Shamans of the Herrera Indians of Cumana "stroked all over the sick man's body, used words of enchantment, licked some joints, and sucked, saying they drew out spirits; took a twig of a certain tree, tickled their own throats with it, until they vomited and bled;

sighed, roared, quaked, stamped, made a thousand faces, sweated for two hours, and at last brought up a sort of thick phlegm, with a little, hard, black ball in the middle of it , which relative of the sick person carried into the field saying, 'Go thy way, Devil.'"[23] The patient is usually amazed and often feels better. The incantations and herbal medicines often have curative properties. But when Stanley Kripner, who is both a scientist and a trained magician, made a formal study of healing ceremonies among primitive tribes, he could account for most of their magic cures through common sleight of hand tricks.

The power of modern wizards relies less on illusion and faith. It comes from science and small advances in areas such as microchip design, genetic engineering, or computer software. Thus, our modern wizards can create billion dollar corporations.

Most employees, from board members to sales and service representatives, are unaware of their archetypal tribal roles, and this also applies to corporate wizards.

Corporations hire their own in-house wizards. They also hire outside consultants, who are seen to have more knowledge and magic than their own employees. Firms like Booz, Allen & Hamilton and McKinsey & Co. are also dens of wizards. Corporations shell out enormous consulting fees to have youthful teams of nerds, waving their magical MBAs, take over their conference rooms, spin out reams of financial runes, interview customers and employees, and then meet with top leaders to foretell their future or recommend reorganizations. Consultants often make the best wizards, since the have the mystique of coming in from outside. One observer said consultants come into your company, ask to borrow your watch, and then tell you what time it is.

In the field of industrial psychology and human resources in general, consultants are often called "headshrinkers." This label represents a kind of dim recognition of the archetypal tribal role that such consultants play in their client tribes.

BURNING THE BITCHES

Early anthropologists recorded a great many magical behaviors used by uncivilized peoples. The North American Indian, eager to kill a bear, would hang

---

23.Spencer, Herbert , op. cit., page 242.

up a rude grass image of one and shoot it, reckoning that this symbolic act would make the real one happen. The native Australians, at a burial ceremony, would observe the direction of the flames and smoke at the burial fire in order to determine what direction to go to find the wicked sorcerer who had killed their kinsman. The Zulu who planned to buy cattle could be seen chewing a piece of wood, in order to soften the heart of the seller with whom he would be dealing.

In the pseudo-science of astrology, similar bits of magical thinking still influence modern men and women. Thus, a man born under the sign of Taurus is thought likely to have a broad brow and thick lips, and to be brutal and unfeeling, and when enraged, violent and furious. If he had been born under the sign of Libra, he would have a just and well-balanced mind.

In a modern, science-oriented culture, people are sometimes squeamish when they are asked to participate in primitive wizard tricks. Nonetheless, one successful device that has been used in team-building exercises does just that. It's called *burning the bitches*.

In prison, the army, and in union meetings, informal bitch sessions can go on for hours and the most eloquent complainers often gain followers and become opposition leaders who work against the formal leadership. Who hasn't seen an employee gathering where the complaints of one or two workers inflamed the entire group and problems which had been small ones suddenly grew into major morale issues? For this reason, corporations should avoid holding any open meetings whose only objective is the airing of complaints — that is like fertilizing the weeds.

Rather, the corporations should use *burning the bitches* sessions to convert complaints into an opportunity to reinforce loyalty. The wizard-consultant gives participants three or four strips of paper and they are asked to write down, on each one, the things that most annoy them about their company or their team. They are instructed to write down the things they most often complain about, the things that really bug them, and then bring their slips of paper to the evening session.

Many participants worry about openly sharing their secret frustrations in front of their fellow workers; but others do it openly and often. They enjoy airing their complaints and often do not realize how it can erode morale and inhibit positive action.

When employees arrive with their slips of paper, they are invited to sit around a campfire. The session begins with an explanation of how negative thoughts and feeling about their company weigh them down like heavy baggage. Considering all their frustrations and complaints as past history, they can start a new chapter by getting rid of the negative baggage. Then, one by one, they are asked to come forward and toss their slips of paper into the fire. Some do it eagerly, relieved that they will not have to share their negative feelings. Others, who were looking forward to airing their frustrations, are more reluctant to let go.

The rest of the session is spent telling stories about times they were most proud of their company, incidents that strengthened their commitment and made them feel proud of their leaders. It is not uncommon at the end of such sessions, with emotions running high and loyalties strengthened, for employees to step forward with moving stories about their experience. One man tells his story of how the company provided insurance for his daughter's leukemia; others praise the company for the support it gave them to continue in school, and so on. These revelations are good marks for the corporate wizard: you can almost feel employees' positive feelings for their company grow.

There is no scientific justification for a relationship between burning the bitches and improved morale, but like a sugar pill, it seems to work.

USE OF ARCHETYPES IN CAREER COUNSELING

Understanding the wizard archetype can often be helpful in areas of career counseling. Sometimes helping someone to understand his or her archetypal role is like removing a cataract from their eyes.

The headshrinker could see that he was a corporate wizard the moment he walked into the room. His granny glasses and wild hair gave him away.

The huge electric utility corporation had hired an industrial psychologist to provide management development and career counseling services to the corporation's directors and vice presidents. The consultant had administered a battery of psychological and intelligence tests and collected ratings of various executive competencies from bosses, subordinates, and peers. He then fed back the results and helped each participant create a two to three year development program that included appropriate development seminars, readings, and rotational assignments.

But when the executive was asked about his aspirations, it was clear that he was unaware of his archetypal role. He wanted to run a large operating division of the corporation.

When the psychologist asked him to tell about some of the accomplishments he was most proud of, he smiled and described a new mathematical model he had created that accurately predicted corporate revenues. Intelligence tests confirmed that he was brilliant. His love of science and particularly mathematics had first surfaced in high school and continued through college and graduate school where he had earned a PhD.

In all large utility corporations, the generals and the armies they lead do battle with the weather. When ever huge storms knock out service, the big trucks roll. Thousands of uniformed linemen literally risk their lives tracking down broken lines and climbing icy poles in order to restore service as quickly as possible. Because customers without electricity can freeze to death, these intrepid warriors take their roles very seriously.

It may have been the status and prestige of the field generals that appealed to the executive. Perhaps he felt his role was peripheral to the mainstream. Many staff executives long to try their hand at leading large groups of line employees.

But this bespectacled wizard had never dealt with unions or fired an employee. He had guided three PhD researchers in the development of various computer models, and his contributions to the organization's strategic planning activities were highly valued by those around him. He did not exercise or show any interest in competitive sports. In his spare time he loved to read and play with his computer. It seemed to the psychologist that he was poorly suited to line management, but because many executives succeed in line positions after long careers in staff roles, and vice versa, the consultant did not discourage him.

He did explain the basic tribal roles in corporations, and when the headshrinker told him he was a wizard, the information seemed to hit him like a thunder bolt. He was deeply pleased, in spite of his stated aspirations.

Understanding archetypal roles and the way an employee's natural talents can best be used to help a tribe grow can be an important element of career counseling. Moving this mathematical wizard into a field office in charge of some troops would have the double negative effect of creating poor line manager and losing the contributions of a good scientist. It is likely that he did not realize the lack of intellectual stimulation in a field office. Within a few months, he would probably have tired of the petty complaints and concrete day to day personnel issues that would be a major element of his job.

A few individuals have enough intelligence and warrior competitiveness to do well in either line or staff rolls. The US military consciously rotates its career officers in order to fully develop their capabilities. It may be that the best corporate warriors are those with enough intelligence to understand and properly integrate the contributions of their various tribal wizards.

Many wizards start their own companies or successfully negotiate their way through layers of management to become CEO. In the process, they usually get experience leading departments of accountants or research scientists, and in other ways develop their leadership skills. They must also develop their ability to persuade customers, board members, Wall Street analysts and employees.

Just as warrior kings such as Arthur learn how to employ the advice of wizards like Merlin, the most effective wizard chiefs team up with ramrod warriors who can be aggressive, decisive, even ruthless in implementing strategies and capturing territory.

Just as the top athletes and warriors are often highly intelligent, so too are the top wizards highly ruthless and competitive as tribal leaders. Bill Gates, and Henry Ford obviously fit this model.

THE EVOLUTION OF TRIBAL WIZARDS

Corporate wizards are scientists, rather than priests. They claim no exclusive pipeline to God. In the agricultural era, the best educated individuals were from religious colleges and universities, but this is no longer the case.

The transformation of wise men and women, men and women of knowledge, from the priests and priestesses of organized religions to scientists represents another profound change in the evolution of human clusters. Corporations rely heavily on both pure science and the applied sciences to create new products, manage their companies and drive tribal growth.

Unlike the castles of Europe, few corporations have chapels as a part of the corporate office complex, and few sales organizations seek the blessings of priests or other holy men prior to launching their annual campaigns.

Even though corporations do not overtly seek help from God, they clearly allow and permit employees of many religions to join their companies. And cases of disruption due to religious conflict among employees are rare. These new tribes tolerate all religions.

Chapter Eight:
The Chief Archetype

Of all the tribal archetypes, that of the chief is the most clear and the easiest to identify. Every human cluster has one. Hundreds of titles such as Czar, President, Chairman, Prime Minister, King, Pope, Queen, Pharaoh, Caesar, Headman, Dalai Lama, Warden, Doge, General, Sila, Chairman, and CEO have been used to identify the person who fills this ancient and enduring role.

The role seems to extend beyond Homo sapiens to animal clusters. It is an anchor point in all dominance hierarchies, referred to by biologists as the Alpha role.

It may even extend in some form to colonizing insects such as ants, termites, and bees where the queen is guarded, protected, and fed a special diet.

In Australia a mammal, a hairless rat, organizes like these colonizing insects. These rodents spend their entire lives underground in elaborate tunnels. A class of smaller and more energetic worker rats feeds rows of fat pink "upper class" rats that lie back like puffy pink carpets in special chambers. The workers also raise food, dig new tunnels, and keep the tunnels clean. A single huge queen gives birth to all the new rats in the colony. She is tended, protected, and fed like the queen bee in a hive.

However deep in phylogeny this role originated, there is no doubt than humans are fascinated and entranced by the individuals who fill the Alpha position. When the president walks through the employee cafeteria, every head turns and every pair of eyes take a peek. When the CEO is in a bad mood, the news filters down quickly through the ranks. The shy employee who finds himself in the elevator with the President might lose his voice or begin to quake in the knees.

In many conglomerates, the CEO and his top team make an annual journey to review the plans and results of their many operating units. The meeting is critical to the leaders of the operating unit. If they present their case well, they may be able to get a slightly larger share of the corporate budget and garner the funding they need to expand their operations. If their result are poor, or there are errors in their data, their unit could be sold off or they might even be replaced. When top corporate leaders are so rarely visible to the employees of far flung operating units, and wield such power, they tend to take on almost mythical god-like aura. In some units, thousands of man hours are spent preparing data, slide shows, and elaborate books full of financial information. They conduct rehearsals of their presentations while managers fire difficult questions at them. The visiting dignitaries are treated to fine dinners, gifts and chauffeured limousine service. One has to wonder whether the CEOs, flattered by the obsequious attention, realize how much time and effort has been diverted away from the primary task of running the business and responding to important customers.

Corporations pay their CEOs obscene amounts: salaries, bonuses, and stock options worth millions. This royal jelly sets up the Alpha role to be the most attractive, the most sought after and competed for in the tribe. Thousands of young executives set their career goals on becoming the CEO and work diligently to get there. They want the modern palaces, estates, ranches, expensive cars, boats and private jets that CEOs enjoy.

Presidents of countries and of corporations are seen as having great powers. They are given credit for things they had nothing to do with, and are blamed for things over which they had no influence. In primitive tribes, disasters such as floods, sickness or deaths, famines or earthquakes were routinely blamed on the chief. But they also got credit for victories in war, good harvests, good hunting and fishing, and expanding tribal territory. They are loved and hated, worshiped and criticized far more than they deserve.

God Kings

During the age of agriculture, the Alpha was seen as a God or as chosen by God. He or she was worshiped, admired, feared, protected by armies, given tributes, and regarded as the father or mother of their tribe or nation-states. The very concept of God, the father in heaven, may condition believers in deference and obedience that makes them better, more compliant participants in the dominance hierarchies of their various human clusters. Kneeling, bowing, averting ones eyes, special forms of address, and elaborate ceremonies which involved displays of deference were and are ubiquitous. When British royalty ventures out of their royal compound, those they are likely to encounter are carefully briefed as to the proper forms of address and how to perform the proper bow.

Special clothing such as purple robes, and props such as umbrellas, scepters, swords, canes, thrones and crowns were all created to identify and honor Alpha. Special architecture from the chief's hut and the White House to elaborate palaces, temples, and cathedrals were and are a consistent feature of every human culture, particularly since the advent of agriculture.

Human tribes trace their histories as a succession of chiefs. From Saul and David in the Bible to Alexander, Hannibal, Hitler and Eisenhower, all seem to hold a special fascination that make them the favorite subjects of biographers. The amount of interest generated by presidents of the United States and the time and effort expended by the press during election campaigns reflect the same trance that grips all participants in all tribes.

Not only did millions of our human ancestors believe their leader was God, or was chosen by God, so also did the leaders believe this about themselves. The belief in the divinity of kings, so prevalent in Europe, must have been immensely seductive to those lucky enough to be born to the right royal parents.

Corporate CEOs still trail these clouds of divine glory. Those who understand the appeal and biological power of the alpha archetype and use it skillfully can dramatically enhance their effectiveness. Those who do not understand it can wreak havoc.

The CEO of a major airline had risen through the ranks of the accounting department. Unfortunately, he did not understand the power of the alpha archetype. He was rather plain in his interests and tastes and far too predictable in his daily work habits. His several thousand employees needed a leader that could inspire them, challenge them to greater performance, and provide a vision that would attract their enthusiastic support. Instead, they had a plain fellow who got to work at precisely the same time each day, wore the ties his wife laid out for him, kept meetings to a minimum, and spent much of his time alone in his office pouring over figures and financial data. He had no idea that his bland personality was limiting and inhibiting his tribe's growth.

It was not easy to persuade him to arrive at the annual management meeting in a helicopter, or to work with a public speaking coach to spice up his presentation. He was hesitant to spend the money and underestimated the impact of a grand entrance. But his employees loved it and he was surprised and delighted by the positive feedback.

Recognizing that everything alpha does, each gesture and facial expression, each speech, each decision, is dramatically magnified by the alpha archetype can help CEOs accomplish more. When valuable employees decide to leave a company, alpha can often save them simply by calling them and asking them to stay. Alpha can cut through months of bargaining to settle labor disputes and negotiations. Alpha can recruit top talent and seal acquisitions by understanding and using the archetypal power of his or her tribal role. Alpha can inspire the sales force, honor tribal elders, and provide visions of the future like no one else.

Employees yearn for alpha to be their hero. They want someone who entertains them and gives them episodes from which they can create a tribal mythology. Having a leader they admire gives them a sense of invincibility and boldness that can drive corporate growth. Conversely, a leader who embarrasses them, makes them feel ashamed, or does not inspire confidence, undermines effort and allegiance.

IDENTIFYING ALPHA

Another indication of our fascination with alphas is the huge body of research, and the hundreds of books and articles on leadership. Almost everyone has an opinion about what makes a good president. Every president or board committee who had to pick a successor has confronted this issue.

In all higher animals the struggle for dominance begins early. The play of young animals results in a dominance hierarchy. Tinbergen[24] discovered that

---

24. Tinbergen, N., *Social Behavior in Animals* (New York: Wiley, 1953).

young geese tend to hitch hike on the dominance of their mothers, but that a reshuffling occurs at adolescence when they leave the protection of the adults. The phenomenon of clusters of adolescent males and females is seen in many, perhaps all, species of higher animals.

In wolf packs, there are dominant females as well as males, and they are frequently not the largest animals. Strength is important, but not sufficient.

Leadership may be hard to define, but we know it when we see it. The high-schooler who becomes the quarterback or gets elected class president may not be the biggest and toughest, but he sure is a leader.

It is not an accident that so many CEOs reveal leadership traits very early in their careers. They were class presidents, captains of their athletic teams, valedictorian, presidents of their fraternity or the youngest vice presidents ever appointed by their companies.

Athletics often play a key role in that they provide a competitive arena where the struggle for dominance can be played out. However, there is a reshuffling of the dominance hierarchy after high school, and again after college when young men and women go through the rite of passage we know as *commencement*. Many of the top athletes and most popular students in high school and college seem to run out of gas in the corporate world. Some of the nerds leave them in the dust.

Some future presidents show an ability to make money at an early age. They launch entrepreneurial ventures or multiply their lawn mowing or house painting businesses by hiring others to do the work.

It has been shown that the ratio of age-to-earnings can be a key predictor. Those who earn more than their age mates at a young age may retain a similar ratio throughout their careers.. In other words, the person who is in the 90th percentile of earnings among age mates at age twenty may still be in the 90th percentile at age fifty.

Like athletics, corporations also provide an arena where dominance hierarchies form and are played out. There is little doubt that intelligence plays a major role. Being an astute politician and knowing how to cultivate mentors and gain the confidence of the board and other top executives is a form of intelligence not measured by current tests. Yet this *social* or *political* intelligence may be particularly critical. Reporting to a vice president who gets fired is less wise than finding a boss who is moving up and then riding his or her coattails.

Confidence and bravado also play a key role. Among the great apes, the individual who can intimidate others by roaring, beating his chest or tearing off the largest tree branches and pounding them on the ground often achieves the alpha role.

Most corporations have good, solid information to rely on when choosing a new leader. They have track records. They know which of their operating units grew most and was most profitable under which candidate, or which candidate sold the largest contracts or built the most talented management team.

Although it is not likely to show up in an interview, alphas may also have a ruthless streak. In defeating a rival, whether it is a competing corporation or an internal competitor, they are willing to play dirty.

Frank Smith, not his real name, was the CFO of a successful dolomite mining corporation. It was a family-owned corporation being run by the son of the founder. Frank knew that the President did not have the undivided support of his brothers and sisters. He also knew that if the family combined forces, they had enough stock to out vote the president.

Frank kept a close watch on the feelings and frustrations of the family. He also met secretly with some investment bankers. When the president promoted his twenty-three-year old son to a vice president position for which he clearly was not qualified, and at the same time transferred a nephew to an undesirable job, several key family members were furious. Frank seized his opportunity. He called a secret meeting with the disgruntled family members and convinced them to sell him their stock.

The president was completely blind-sided when Frank fired him. He could not believe it. His closest, most trusted advisor had gone around him and secretly acquired a controlling interest in the company.

Frank went on to be a highly effective president of the company. The ruthless streak he had employed successfully to buy the company also helped him outflank and defeat some key competitors.

Nature obviously produces far more alphas than it needs and the struggle for dominance in corporations pit talented men and women against each other in ways that help to assure that a top quality individual ascends to the alpha position.

COMPENSATION AND THE DOMINANCE HIERARCHY

Compensation consultants can tell you that every corporation has separate compensation schemes for hourly vs. salaried employees. It seems to be a given. Executives also have separate compensation programs that include large bonuses, stock options and lists of executive perks that may include cars, country club memberships, box seats at sporting and cultural events, paid moving expenses, and a variety of other expenses both routine and luxurious. The compensation traditions in major corporations reflect, parallel and contribute to the same sort of class stratification observed in other cultures. Separate executive, salaried and hourly pay schemes create classes that are like the nobles, soldiers, and serfs that can be identified in various traditional European, Chinese and Indian class systems.

Many CEOs are too embarrassed by their own pay to ask their board for a raise; so they hire consulting firms. Consultants who understand the game can always find survey data that shows the top executives need a raise. When the pay increases are recommended to the board's compensation committee on Peat Marwick or Booz Allen letterhead, they are likely to be approved. Wealthy CEOs hire consultants to make them more wealthy, especially by designing stock option programs.

It is essential that the compensation executives receive follows the perceived dominance hierarchy precisely. This is an almost eerie replay of the primitive tribal ceremony wherein an astonishingly obese chief would sit on a scale while his supplicants piled gold, jewelry and other tribute on a counter balance trying to equal his weight.

All of these dramatic imbalances of wealth reflect tribal dominance hierarchies. These great displays are clear symbols of the power of Alpha. Whether a tribe measures its wealth in horses, wives, cattle, pigs, yams, grain bins, acres of cropland or stock options, Alpha gets the most. Sub chiefs and vice presidents are next. The distribution of wealth follows and strengthens the dominance hierarchy.

Some corporations boast about having achieved a new, less "top-down" form of organization which allows workers more responsibility and freedom to make decisions. They use quality circles to solve problems and strip out layers of management to reduce bureaucracy and encourage employee participation. Many have succeeded in improving productivity and profit margins. Some even eliminate titles and refer to all employees as "team members." However, despite the claims that are made, the leveling effect does not extend to the pay scheme for CEOs and Vice Presidents. The distribution of proceeds from the profits of the hunt mirrors the pecking order of the corporate tribes. It shows that dominance hierarchies are alive and well.

As much as we humans want to believe that we are free of the laws of nature and can create whatever kinds of organizations we wish, there is no escape from the dominance hierarchy, and no human organization can endure for very long without someone in the alpha position.

Sometimes, when two companies merge, they try to smooth over the tough question of who will be the new president of the merged firm by creating an "Office of the President."

Predictably, the two chiefs will have a difficult time parceling out responsibilities, determining which employees will be promoted, and deciding how to spend money and divide the budget pie. They will need more than team building to blend two very different tribes, each with its own history, style, and clientele; and each with its own chief. Evidence shows that companies without a single leader are unstable. The "old-fashioned, top-down, military style" of leadership works for some, while others style themselves as a group of equal colleagues — but the pay scale still reflects the reality of the hierarchy. Soon after a merger like this, one of the two presidents usually gets an offer and leaves, once again to run his or her own ship.

When it comes to pecking orders and the alpha role, nature seems to abhor a vacuum. All human clusters have them. And when explorers encountered strange tribes in Africa and South America they did not ask, "How is your tribe organized?" They said, "Take me to your leader."

Alpha and Sexual Appetite

As the memoirs of Bill Russell, the basketball legend, demonstrate, great warriors can attract women by the thousands. The phenomenon is disturbingly parallel to what is observed in other higher mammals. The strongest and most powerful males attract more than their fare share of females and contribute more of their DNA to the succeeding generation than others do. In many higher mammals, males who are not strong enough to capture and control a harem or a breeding territory contribute nothing to the succeeding generation. This focused passing of only the strongest animal's genetic traits obviously contributes to the survival of their species.

Howard Hughes, Elvis Presley, King Solomon, politicians, rock stars and other powerful and wealthy men have demonstrated huge sexual appetites. This is particularly evident in cultures where polygamy is practiced. The harems in China, Iran, Egypt, and Africa were largest where the leaders were most powerful and wealthy.

It is possible, perhaps even probable, that hormones such as testosterone play a role in both warrior behavior and sexual appetite. If these traits are truly linked, men who rise to power in organizations may also have greater sexual appetites. They may also have more opportunities for and more actual sexual encounters than others.

There is little doubt that religious beliefs can and do modify behavior, including sexual behavior. A belief in monogamy and conviction that sex with someone other than one's spouse is a sin prevents the unencumbered expression of the sexual appetites of many devout and powerful men. In some corporations, employees who have sex with other employees, and are discovered, are quickly terminated. However, in other corporations the widespread taboo against "dipping one's pen in company ink" is more or less ignored.

If those who rise to power have a greater sexual appetite than others, the renowned sexual activities of so many American presidents, including John Kennedy and William Clinton, are understandable, perhaps even predictable. To screen out possible candidates for top leadership positions because of their active sexual appetites may be foolish, if not dangerous. It may mean inadvertently screening out other warrior-like traits that contribute to leadership effectiveness, especially in competitive situations.

ALPHA AND VISION

The term *vision* has become loaded and hot with meaning. Like *intelligence* and *creativity*, it is now regarded as an indispensable trait of the effective CEO. Yet, its meaning is often obscure. To the optometrist, the term *vision* has a very clear and specific meaning, but the religious mystic has a very different definition usually involving contact with spirits or glimpses of the future.

The mysticism with which the term *vision* is presented makes it seem even more appealing to many executives. They wonder if some CEOs have more talent or skill at seeing into the future than others, and they want to develop this skill. Corporations run programs that draw on all sorts of mythology, role-playing and story-telling to get the juices flowing, then organize the participants into discussion groups to generate ideas. The end results are not greatly different from those achieved in the typical strategic planning session, but it makes everybody feel good. Most major corporations conduct some form of strategic planning sessions annually.

The way to take the mystery out of the term *vision* is to call it what it is, a plan. A vision is simply a plan. Perhaps a vision is the germ of an idea that is then fashioned into a plan by adding specific action steps and target dates.

One day, many years ago, when Southern Airways (long since acquired), was just getting started, Frank Hulse, the founder and president received a call from the manager of maintenance. "Take a look out your window," he said. Frank strolled over to the window and saw a strange sight: a weird-looking contraption was landing on the runway. It sounded like a threshing machine and its appendages looked more like boards than wings. As it taxied toward Southern's maintenance hangar, every mechanic on the shop floor stopped working and stared at the flying jitney. A young man climbed out and said, "Take me to your leader," or words to that effect. It was George Gross, a Georgia farm boy who had built the homemade plane with his brothers. He had flown it to Atlanta to look for a job and after Frank Hulse took a closer look at his plane, he hired him on the spot. It was a smart decision.

George rose quickly through the ranks and eventually became President. In a time when the term *vision* had not yet become fashionable, George presented his *plan* to his leadership team. "We are going to double our fleet, build a new corporate headquarters and a new maintenance hangar, and triple the number of our employees in the next three years," he said calmly. "And we are going to do all this with someone else's money."

Everyone was astonished; but soon there was a model of the new headquarters building proudly displayed in the lobby of the dilapidated office. The excitement and the energy level of the managers and employees was palpable. Over the next several months, the plan took shape. Everything the boss had predicted came to pass and the employees felt proud and invincible.

In this example, the model of the new administration building did more to translate the CEO's vision into something concrete than anything else; and when the concept of *vision* is considered, its companion concept must be *focus*. The

CEO must make the vision clear enough and compelling enough so that thousands of employees can see it clearly.

Whose vision is projected, and how consistently, can make all the difference. A struggle for control usually ensues unless the hierarchy is clear, and a single visionary can set the direction. Experience proves that it is difficult it is to perform even simple tasks without *vision*, and conversely, how simple it can be when all team members are pulling in the same direction.

New ideas or directions, presented by a respected leader, can generate immense excitement and effort in a large group of corporate employees. It can focus the energies of thousands of dedicated, hard working tribesmen and women and when they see the plan begin to take shape and move from flip charts to reality, the motivational impact is extremely powerful.

Many times, there is no difficulty in generating ideas. A far greater challenge is sorting through the extensive list of ideas and proposed projects to select those which stand the best chance of being implemented successfully. Furthermore, it is always difficult to stick with a project and provide the sustained work and tedious effort needed to make it succeed. Creative types are notorious for losing interest once the ideas have been hatched. They want to create again rather than patiently nurture an idea into a mature product. A creative CEO can sometimes wreak havoc on an organization by too frequently shifting gears, reorganizing, changing leaders or losing patience with the less interesting work of disseminating a new produce or service and selling it well to all the corporation's customers.

In this respect, it may be unwise to expect every CEO to be a visionary or to regard having "vision" as an indispensable trait. Being bold, being an intelligent strategist, and being able to drive the ongoing development of a good, practical, doable plan and applying the discipline necessary to stick to that plan may be a far more important skill.

THE ALPHA ROLE

Alpha, the chief, represents an essential reference point that, like the keystone of an arch, is essential to the stability of all tribes, ancient and modern.

In the San Blas islands off the coast of Panama, the Cuna Indians have been very cautious about opening up to the modern world. Their social organization follows the same hierarchy as the most up-to-date multinational corporation.

Each island has its own Sila, or chief. There are regional Silas, like regional VPs, for groups of island, and a Grand Sila for the entire San Blas nation. (Although officially part of Panama, they see themselves as an independent nation.) The alpha role, in this case called Sila, is essential for tribal leadership, and as a linking pin for larger organization clusters.

The death of the alpha is usually a tribal catastrophe. During that part of the agricultural age when alpha was seen as God, there could be no recovery. Thus, when Cortes captured Montezuma with a handful of Spanish soldiers, all his massive army, thousands of Aztecs, were immobilized by fear. During skirmishes with tribes in Africa, various European adventurers discovered that if they could identify and kill the tribal leader, the battle would be over. The shock to the tribe was devastating.

In books, in the movies, on television, at school, and at work, we see the Alpha role played out over and over again. The daily attention to England's royal family demonstrates how much theater is involved. Just as the audience judges Mel Gibson when he plays Hamlet, so also do employees judge the performance of each CEO they encounter. This judgment is often made through a lens of excessive admiration and excessive fear. Each decision, each action taken, each employee fired or promoted, each quarterly report of profits or losses, each indiscretion, each win and each defeat is magnified.

When the chief understands the alpha role, and plays it well, he or she can leverage his or her own capabilities by inspiring followers. They can build allegiance, encourage creativity and stimulate extra effort. As many CEOs will attest, they can be far more persuasive as Alpha than when they are playing other roles, such as husband or father. When the chief plays the alpha role clumsily or rudely, or does not understand the power of the chief archetype or use it wisely, he or she can dampen allegiance, and limit the energy employees are willing to expend.

Employees want their leader to be heroic. They know that if the tribe grows they can count on a steady income, and maybe even earn a bonus. They want to believe that their president has superhuman qualities and capabilities. They want showmanship and flamboyance, as well as intelligence and stability. Because millions of employees are now shareholders of their companies, they also want a leader who will increase the value of their stock and provide a secure retirement.

Chapter Eight: The Chief Archetype

Some of the essential traits, for example financial acumen, may be new to the corporate tribal mutation. Skill at making and winning war appears to be less essential than before; but most of the traits and talents essential for leadership in earlier tribes, including those of the agricultural era, still exist.

CHAPTER NINE:
THE COUNCIL OF ELDERS

In 1897, Herbert Spencer reported about the councils of elders found among the Arafuras (Papuan Islanders), tribes of the Todas, Bodos and Dhimals, and North American tribes such as the Comanches and Iroquois.

> In districts of ancient Central America...the government was carried on by an elective council of old men who appointed a war chief; and this war chief, if suspected of plotting against the safety of the commonwealth, or for the purpose of securing supreme power in his own hands, was rigorously put to death by the council.[25]

In tribes both primitive and modern, groups of elders, usually but not always men, provide counsel, advice, review of plans, and guidance to alpha and their tribe. Usually these elders are past the point of competing for the alpha position and can be trusted to have the welfare of the entire tribe in mind; but this is not always the case. Some board members who have struggled unsuccessfully through their entire careers to become CEO seize upon their board membership to finally exercise the power that had eluded them. They ask for special presentations and reports, try to get groups of employees reporting to them, and are excessively watchful and critical of the CEO. They become involved in the day-to-day operations of their companies, second guess management decisions,

---

25. Spencer, Herbert, *The Principles of Sociology*, (New York: D. Appleton and Company, 1897). Vol. II-I pp367-368).

and aggravate the political maneuvering for power and succession. Some of them harbor hidden agendas to replace the CEO and, indeed, it is not unusual to see this happen.

In corporate tribes, seats on the board become levers for control and are powerful bargaining chips during merger and acquisition negotiations. The by-laws for replacing board members, selecting new ones and determining their terms of office become critical elements in changing the balance of power.

If the by-laws allow it, one person may gain a controlling share of the stock and then personally select each board member. He can even ask a board member to step aside. He can serve as both CEO and Chairman of the Board. In such a case, even if he picks seasoned executives who can direct business to the firm, board meetings can become pointless. The board member who is flattered at being selected may be unlikely to disagree with the CEO or try to change his mind on any issue.

In the tribe we know as the United States, a key council of elders is the Supreme Court. Members serve for life or until they become too old or too unhealthy to continue. They cannot be fired or replaced by a sitting president. They are presumed to be wise men and women who put the welfare of the entire nation above political partisanship. They represent an important balance of power that adds strength and stability to the tribe. It is tempting to give credit to the founding fathers for inventing this important council of elders, but in fact it is typical of other councils in tribes throughout the earth.

When the time comes for Alpha to be replaced, it is the council of elders who makes it happen. Often, one of them invites the CEO to lunch and acts as the kindly Dutch uncle to deliver the bad new. It is curious to note how easily many CEOs surrender when this approach is taken, particularly since many of them fought with such energy and resilience to maintain their position when attacked by others.

Many ambitious men and women long for the day they become CEO because they imagine they will suddenly acquire freedom to implement their plans and do all the things they could not do as Vice President. They unhappily discover that the old men and women above them did not go away. They must still operate with others looking over their shoulders, second guessing them and criticizing their decisions and actions. The need for working effectively with older, more experienced tribesmen and women is critical for anyone who aspires to the alpha position. Tribal survival and growth clearly benefits from the

Chapter Nine: The Council of Elders

wisdom accumulated in the council of elders. The best elders are those who have been CEOs themselves. The worst are those who are in no mood to sit on the sidelines, who are driven by a hidden agenda, or who seek to replace alpha.

Professional associations such as those that serve dentists, psychologists, engineers, and chemists often choose board members to represent various factions of their membership. For example, the board may include representatives from academia, from corporate life, or from pure research. The result can be a rich mix, but it does not necessarily function effectively as a council of elders.

Boards of volunteer organizations such as orchestras, art institutes, and ballet companies can be particularly contentious and political. All board meetings become arenas for political maneuvering, but when status-conscious volunteers with limited leadership experience get involved, the result can be chaotic.

Only when scandals erupt in the open can one see how much the board of directors can be prisoners of the CEO-controlled system, or vice versa. Especially in the nonprofit arena, it is not uncommon to find a situation where the chief executive (usually an Executive Director) is hampered by a board of directors that does not play its tribal role properly. One faction of the board may be calling for the chief's resignation, while others feel that his performance is adequate and that he was quite well-suited to his position.

It may become apparent that the board of directors is not acting as a council of elders. Young, aggressive and ambitious middle managers with strong opinions about how the organization should be run are likely to succumb to the urge to compete, or to exercise their power inappropriately. Replacing the chief would demonstrate their influence. And it is safer to exercise such impulses from a board position than at the corporations where they worked full time.

The best and most effective corporate councils of elders, as their name implies, are made up of true elders, men and women who have become seasoned through many years of experience. They are individuals who have no personal ambitions or private agendas to fulfill but are free to act in the interest of the tribe as a whole. They know how to coach, advise, and encourage without yielding to the temptation to take over. They don't need the money. They can be fair and impartial judges of various compensation plans and pay outs.

When reviewing plans and strategies, they can explain how similar plan in their own companies succeeded or failed. They can often introduce the CEO into new relationships, alert the corporation to talented executives who may be looking for a change, and through their extensive contacts, provide information about potential mergers and acquisitions.

The role of elder, and the Council of Elders, is ancient and enduring. Their existence provides balance and stability for the tribes they serve.

Chapter Ten:
The Troops

The stratification of human cultures is another embarrassing fact of history. The untouchables of India, peons and serfs in Europe, slaves and sharecroppers of pre-Civil War United States all illustrate the lowest rung of status and wealth in agricultural societies. In 1897, Edward B. Tylor observed:

> In the warfare of rude races, it is to be noticed how fighting for quarrel or vengeance begins to pass into fighting for gain. Among some tribes the captives, instead of being slain, are brought back for slaves, and especially set to till the ground. By this agriculture is much increased, and also a new division of society takes place, to be seen still arising among such warlike tribes as the Caribs, where the captives with their children come to form a hereditary lower class. Thus we see how in old times the original equality of men broke up, a nation dividing into an aristocracy of warlike freemen, and an inferior labouring caste. Also forays are made for the warriors to bring home wives, who are the slaves and property of their captors.[26]

In the agricultural era, this class structure expanded as large numbers of humans were captured in wars. They worked on estates of landowners, built pyramids in Egypt and Central America, and castles and fortifications in Europe and China.

---

26. Taylor, Edward B., *Anthropology — An Introduction to the Study of Man and Civilization* (New York: D. Appleton & Company, 1897).

In times of war, they became foot soldiers. Landowners of the largest estates were often called upon to provide troops when their country was at war. Some were so effective in training and equipping their men that they became warlords and could join the forces of whatever side would pay them the most. In Europe, those who fought well were rewarded with land grants and those who did not perform well on the battlefield could have their land, and their men, taken away.

The troops were poorly educated, had few resources, and little or no chance of penetrating the barriers that kept them in their place.

In the earliest factories of the industrial era, workers were paid in company credit slips, lived in company-owned houses and bought their groceries and supplies in company-owned stores. After the bills for living expenses were paid, workers were usually still in debt. Like Southern share croppers, indentured servants, and the crews on fishing and whaling vessels, those working for the early corporations found that the Company had ways to keep them from escaping.

The practices of flogging unruly sailors and putting children to work in factories and sweatshops were still common in Western societies as late as 1910. That this was accepted by society at large reflected a set of attitudes and beliefs in the God-given superiority of the ruling classes that was thoroughly entrenched in the minds of landowners and stockholders, and still exists in more subtle ways to this day. It was these indignities that inspired the writings of Marx and Engels and fueled revolutions in France and Russia.

Modern military organizations perpetuate this stratification. Officers ordinarily have a college degree, come from relatively affluent families and are sent to leadership and officer training schools. The troops are known as *enlisted* men and women. They take positions with less responsibility, receive less pay, wear different uniforms and are expected to give frequent demonstrations of deference to their superiors by saluting and obeying each command.

This class structure has survived intact in the corporate tribal mutation. What we refer to as "the working classes" are as *hourly, blue collar, union,* or *non-exempt* employees as opposed to the office workers and the newer breed of the "knowledge workers," who collectively constitute the modern labor class. That's something more obvious in the European model where even in its most dilute form, the British, the class-based party system is built along the lines of Tories versus Labour. In most, perhaps all, corporations these employees have separate pay structures, less vacation time, less pay and fewer perks than those in the management. Where a college degree is required for salaried or management positions, hourly employees often need only a high school diploma.

Depending on the position on the job chart, they may work in cozy offices, as low level data entry, in factory settings or outdoors. Their jobs often require hard physical labor or repetitive motions, and possibly exposure to dangerous situations and the elements. In early corporations they were not treated much better than slaves, but as unions and labor laws emerged and labor-saving machines were created, working conditions and pay levels have improved. The *troops* in modern corporations often achieve lifestyles that are financially far more secure than the serfs of the agricultural era (who usually lived on the brink of destitution and had no realistic options to improve their situation). When all goes well, modern union workers may be able to earn enough to own their own homes, a couple of cars, maybe even a boat or a cabin in the woods.

But, just as strict and separate gender roles are maintained in a family that sets out to reproduce itself by the mean of procreation, so too are the rigid barriers that separate class stratifications between the employers and employees. Individuals from humble backgrounds whose parents were hourly, blue collars workers can rise to top level corporate positions just as many sons and daughters of top corporate executives have slipped to non-management careers, individuals paths can follow individual destinies the class distinction remains as valid today as a thousand years ago. Only the nature of work has changed.

Where the daily work of employees on the lowest rungs of the status ladder were often back breaking, onerous and tedious, much of it now requires greater skill and less sweat. (Operating a trenching machine requires more skill and less sweat than digging a trench with a shovel.) Wherever large numbers of laborers were needed, labor-saving machines have been invented with the result that whole categories of mindless, back-breaking jobs have been eliminated. One can even say that to some extent, new jobs which require greater skill and are far more challenging intellectually have replaced the mindless drudgery that characterized jobs of earlier industrial employees.

In the most advanced industrialized countries, one can say that the new demands for new skills has replaced the *masses* of the lower ranks with an educated population. Reflecting the increasing demand for knowledgeable workers, the 2000 US census shows how rapidly and dramatically the *masses* which once populated the lowest rungs of the socio-economic ladder are being educated. In 1900, only 11% of 14- to 17-year-olds were in school. By 2000, that number had jumped to 93%. Those who had graduated from high school had risen from 13% to 83%. Unfortunately, the United States in the last 20 years has gone countertrend, in its attempt to roll back 100 years of progress achieved by the labor movement.

Differences in education that once separated socioeconomic classes can be reduced by judicious use of television and the Internet. An optimistic Marshall McLuhan pointed out that, in the age of television, sending your child to school represents an interruption in his or her education. Unfortunately, again, we witness a 20-year manifest counter-culture takeover of television as a tool for education by the utmost commercialization and politicization of its content by business interests (especially in the United States). True, the latest discoveries of science are as likely to be reported on television as in the classroom. True, factory workers who watch television can be equally informed on current events as the CEO — whether by Robert Murdoch's Fox channel or Time Warner's CNN. But all the television programs in the world can not blur the distinction between the masters of television and the workers, as consumers of television.

Some may say that stockownership offers the greatest opportunity for employees' emancipation as workers can now become minority stockholders. Yet, ultimately, despite employees' owning a major chunk of the company at United Airlines, management had the discretion to lay off tens of thousands of workers when that became necessary.

Most hourly workers, particularly those who gain seniority, are proud of their status and their basic role in helping their companies grow and prosper. They tend to be suspicious, even scornful of the "suits" who occasionally walk through the shop floor. Some union employees and hourly workers may feel insulted by the idea that their role evolved from slave and serf classes of the agricultural era; but an awareness of these common origins may help all employees at all levels continue the push or even speed up the process of making their jobs more humane.

* * *

These, then are the corporate archetypes: gatherers, hunters (including scouts), wizards, chiefs, elders and the troops. In the agricultural era, these fundamental roles were further subdivided. Some hunters and gatherers who were unlucky enough to be conquered by opposing armies became slaves or serfs. The generals and land owners who were victorious became barons and earls, and after a few generations they as well as their servant/slaves forgot how it all started and grew to accept the status hierarchy as the natural order of things, ordained by God. Tribal wizards became the priests and holy men of organized religions.

The complexity of modern corporations has forced further subdivisions. The role of hunter has split into sales, manufacturing and marketing, each with its own specialists. Still, like the branches and twigs of the evolution tree Darwin described, all corporate jobs can be traced back to their tribal roots.

Some individuals who begin to see the tribal roots of modern corporations more clearly may fall into the trap of romanticizing the noble savage. There is much to admire. The beauty of tribal art, the healing powers of tribal shamans, the impressive bonding of families, the strength and beauty of hunters and gatherers, their love of the earth and its animals, their thorough knowledge of their territories, and their enduring survival skills are all admirable.

In his book *Indian Givers*,[27] Jack Weatherford reminds us of the immense debt we owe to the native people of the Americas. His research indicates that 60% of the foods eaten in the world today, including potatoes, chocolate, and chilies, were first harvested by the Indians of the Americas. Many aspects of modern medicine, agriculture, architecture, and ecology trace their roots to native American cultures. The great treasures of gold, silver, and precious gems unearthed by natives of the new world and shipped to Europe created great empires.

But less than two hundred year ago, when Lewis and Clark traveled across what is now northern Wyoming and Montana, they encountered Blackfoot women with gaping holes in their faces. Their noses had been cut off as a punishment for adultery. The shocking savagery of primitive tribes, the irrational fears of evil spirits which often controlled their daily lives, the sacrifice of

---

27. Weatherford, Jack, *Indian Givers* (New York: N.Y., Fawcett Columbine, 1988).

children, the killing and blood feuds with enemy tribes, the lack of basic medical care and the poverty which many tribes endured are not admirable.

Where modern men and women can learn a lot from the study of earlier tribal adaptations, the central message of this book goes in the opposite direction. The process of evolution and the new corporate tribes are releasing us from poverty, disease, and hopefully, the barbaric blood and tears of tribal war.

Chapter Eleven:
On Becoming a Corporate Tribe

Recognizing that corporations are, in fact, evolved tribes, is an eye-opener. Each has a unique history, some spanning several generations. Each has its heroes and survival stories. Corporate tribes each have their own marketing territories and customer herds.

Functioning well as a corporate tribe does not entail making massive changes in policies or practices, just a new awareness of a corporation's true essence. When all of the hunters and gatherers understand their roles and perform them well, and when all the wizards and war chiefs do their thing, the tribe will prosper.

Seeing oneself as a tribesman or tribeswoman may not seem like a profound change from seeing oneself as a corporate employee; but when employees can be brought to recognize the archetypal role they are being asked to fill, and to accept it, then they may even find playing that role well for the tribe can be a renewing experience.

Savvy corporations will discover that it is easier, more concrete, to generate loyalty to the tribe than to an abstract balance sheet or a four-page legal description or to whatever else defines the true essence of a corporation.

CEOs come and go. Employees are added and subtracted. Even owners change, and the name above the door, but the tribe remains. In acquired companies, most of the employees keep their jobs — especially if their tribe has been profitable.

Some employees retire and others move up to replace them. The machinery and equipment often do not skip a beat. Tribes seem to endure while the people and personalities change. Tribes are the self-perpetuating survival entities of Homo sapiens.

Gatherer employees who are not aware of their tribal roles may perform their jobs mechanically, putting in their time and picking up their paychecks; they may not realize how their performance as food-getters and nurturers helps or hurts their tribe members.

Most sales reps do have a dim recognition of their role as tribal hunters. They use hunting and military jargon in describing their work; but sometimes sales forces get stale. Their jobs become routine. Their weapons get dull. They lose their enthusiasm and competitive fierceness, and the result is eroding market share. Clarifying their tribal role can sometimes spark new enthusiasm and generate new fierceness.

Relatively few corporate scientists and professionals see themselves as tribal wizards, but recognizing their archetypal roles can help clarify what is expected of them and can be an important means of motivating them to do what the corporation needs. Those who do not keep up with technology or scientific advances, and those who do not stay current with professional knowledge, for example changes in accounting and tax laws, can hurt their companies. And the path to becoming a great corporate wizard, one that travels from one corporation to another and gets paid for his or her knowledge or expertise, is easier when one understands the wizard archetype.

Most CEOs understand their leadership role. It is difficult and demanding. CEOs must dance for the Board of Directors and major stockholders, sing to the investment houses, and play the Big Cheese for customers and employee groups. Mostly, they must work effectively with small teams of executives and managers to formulate plans, solve problems, review results and make the hiring, buying and strategic decisions required to grow their company. Their speeches can inspire and motivate employee groups. Their delegated decisions fan out across the corporation and provide focus and direction for thousands of hours of coordinated effort.

Unfortunately, few CEOs understand the tribal and animal roots of the alpha role or that the cluster of humans they lead is an evolved tribe. When they learn to use the attributes of the position properly, they, too, find they are working with sharper, better weapons.

Chapter Eleven: On Becoming a Corporate Tribe

The Actualized Corporate Tribe

What would a corporation be like, if all its employees were fully aware of their tribal roles and performed them well?

The hunters would be bringing home lots of bacon, enough to feed the tribe's employees, its stockholders, and provide funds for research, acquisitions, new product development, and new technology. Their weapons, those persuasive materials they carry in their briefcases, would be very sharp, even devastating. The tribe's marines would be winning market share from key competitors in their frontier areas and the hunter-warriors would be defending their home territories well from invaders.

The scouts (marketing, intelligence) would be showing the tribe where the hunting is best, what key competitors are doing, as well as helping the hunters be most effective. They would be creating clever traps and snares to lure customers in areas of store design and advertising campaigns.

All the gatherers would recognize their food-getting role and actively work to generate sales, nurture customers, and maintain effective working relationships with fellow employees.

The wizards would be finding ways to give their tribe a competitive advantage, a scientific breakthrough, a great new product, a brilliant financial or legal maneuver.

The CEO would be dancing and singing persuasively for various audiences, while prowling for acquisitions and alliances. Gathering and absorbing information from all sources, he or she would be building and husbanding the tribe's financial and human resources, especially its leadership team. The CEO would direct the deployment of resources, impress and reassure major customers and resolve internal conflicts. He or she would understand the alpha role, take full advantage of its ancient tribal power, and play it skillfully so that employees would be committed to their leader as well as to their missions. The CEO would orchestrate tribal gatherings and provide an arena for honoring the elders as well as recognizing outstanding performances from hunters, gatherers, troops and wizards.

The Board would see clearly their role as the council of elders. They would continue to monitor the chief and when needed, select a new one. They would review over all plans and progress of the tribe, approve public offerings, acquisition, and compensations plans, and provide counsel and advice as such councils have always done.

In the daily wars for gaining and controlling market share, the corporation that is aware of it tribal essence, and uses the knowledge well, will have a clear advantage over competitors who are naive about their own anthropology.

PART TWO

WORLD CULTURES VS. THE CORPORATE CULTURE

Chapter Twelve:
The World's Various Cultures

The dictionary defines *culture* as "the customary beliefs, social forms, and material traits of a racial, religious or social group."[28] For many generations social scientists have used this definition and when they described the Chinese, Hawaiian, or French cultures, their meaning was clear. In anthropology, the term "culture" refers to large human clusters with similar languages, religious beliefs, world views, art styles, home construction, food-getting methods, costumes, and ceremonies. When scientists refer to the Japanese culture, they mean the entire island nation of Japan and its worldwide diaspora, as well as the language, religions, art styles, customs, and common beliefs of individuals who grew up in Japan or have relatives there who transmitted these cultural elements.

A few generations ago, before airplanes, computers, and television began to scramble and mix human clusters, travelers had no difficulty recognizing a different culture. When they crossed some border or entered a new country, they encountered strange-looking people, curious ceremonies, strange languages, unfamiliar religions, new foods and exotic costumes.

Readers of *National Geographic* have always been fascinated and entertained by the curious images of men with painted faces and bare-chested women; but cultural differences go much deeper than these surface appearances. Some cul-

---

28.*Webster's Ninth New Collegiate Dictionary* (Springfield Massachusetts, Merriam-Webster Inc. 1989)

tures developed belief systems that justified the systematically killed female infants. Many have sacrificed thousands of their own people to their gods. Millions of average men and women have died in wars that have resulted from cultural clashes. Most, perhaps all, wars have religious or racial components and cultures that become dominant seem eager to spread their particular beliefs and stamp out weaker cultures.

Joel Kotkin[29] brilliantly describes how the worldwide diaspora of certain especially widely spread cultures, such as the British, the Jews, the Chinese, and the Indians, have established multinational economic networks and trading relationships based on ethnic identity and tribal trust which provide the basic building blocks and power centers of the new global economy. Significantly, Kotkin asserts that these global tribes now share a common passion for technology and a belief in scientific progress, and that the impact of these dispersed cultures has had, and will continue to have profound impact on the economy of the twenty-first century.

Because cultures differed so widely, and these differences were so obvious, there was little or no controversy in how the term culture was defined.

CORPORATE CULTURE

When Deal and Kennedy wrote their book *Corporate Culture*,[30] the phrase had legs. It took off and within a few months consultants and business executives all over the world were analyzing their organizations in attempts to define their culture.

Deal and Kennedy suggested that each corporation had its own unique culture, and they went on to define four general types or categories: the Tough Guy, Macho culture; the Work Hard/Play Hard culture; the Bet-Your-Company culture; and the Process Culture. They provide instructions on how to diagnose cultures as well as how to change them.

The new definitions of corporate culture now being bandied about vary substantially, but a common theme has been reduced to: "shared values, beliefs, and assumptions." It can be and is being applied to very small groups. Some

---

29. Kotkin, Joel, op. cit.
30. Deal, Terrence E. & Kennedy, Allan A., *Corporate Cultures The Rites and Rituals of Corporate Life* (Reading, Massachusetts: Addison-Wesley Publishing Company, 1982).

recent writers have referred to departments within corporations as "subcultures." Do two or three people with shared values, beliefs, and assumptions have their own culture? Not quite!

Perhaps the term "culture" should have some elasticity, but to use it in such a narrow context changes the concept entirely and only generates confusion. No wonder many corporations have trouble understanding and defining their own culture.

The concept of "corporate cultures," with its pleasant alliteration, has captured the imagination of so many that to suggest that individual corporations have no separate cultures may border on blasphemy. Nevertheless, the more corporations one looks at, the more one sees that it is true. *Corporations all share the same culture.* Individual corporations clearly do have their own separate and unique tribal customs, but they do not have their own unique cultures.

The Real Corporate Culture

When the old definition of culture is applied more broadly to all corporate activity, all over the earth, it not only works well, it explains and demonstrates that the real *corporate culture* is spreading like a layer of frosting on a cake, covering a broad variety of older ethnic and religious cultures with a new language, new tribal regalia, new kinds of hunting and gathering methods and techniques, new building styles and materials, and a new set of values and beliefs. Beneath the surface of the new corporate culture there are many ancient cultures, many languages, many religions, and many ethnic groups.

The real corporate culture has its own language. The dictionary of corporate terminology has been expanded dramatically over the past two or three generations since these new tribal mutation took root and began to flourish. Acronyms such as CEO, IBM, NYSE, MIS, GE, EDP, and VP have become common elements of the language of the corporate tribesperson. Words and phrases such as blue collar, president, inventory, price fixing, insider trading, focus group, telemarketing, database, downsizing, outplacement, stock option, acquisition, quality circles, mutual funds, and golden handcuffs are all part of the language of the corporate culture. To really understand a culture, one must master the language and this common sense principle applies to the Chinese, Bantu, and Italian cultures as well as to the new corporate culture.

Line up a Masai warrior, an Irishman, an Arab, and an Eskimo and even a child could tell from the way they were dressed that each represented a different culture — unless, of course, they were dressed in their corporate regalia. When someone joins a corporate tribe, he must take on the costume of the global corporate culture, the now ubiquitous suit, shirt and tie (or equivalent). In any airport in the world, the people who are dressed in this "uniform" are assumed to be a part of the global corporate culture: a corporate tribesperson. There may be tribal variations, such as the always quoted blue suit of the IBM executive; but contrary to the claim that each corporation has its own cultural dress standards and style, it is the similarity in appearance from corporation to corporation which is most remarkable.

Anthropologists have noted that the way buildings are constructed varies from culture to culture. The Navaho and Hopi build pueblos, the Algonquins long houses, the nomadic Sioux the familiar cone-shaped tepees. All cultures employ available materials. If, as Deal, Kennedy and a host of others propose, each corporation has its own unique culture, why then do the buildings and office spaces of so many corporations look so much alike? One tribe can move into a space vacated by another and all that it requires to start functioning is to change the name above the door. Office buildings in nearly every country show a similarity in building styles and materials; this, too, points to the emergence of a new common culture, one that transcends and adds a layer onto all the diverse cultures that went before.

Even the new definition of "shared values, beliefs and assumptions" does not differentiate one corporation from another very effectively. If a deck of cards were created, each with a different corporation's values statements printed on it, the similarity would be far more impressive than the differences. Most of them would mention world class products or services, or their commitment to quality and their customers. One would have great difficulty matching the card to its appropriate corporation.

The notion that a skilled consultant or a new president can change a corporation's culture also suggests a lack of understanding of the depth and strength of the glue that binds the values, beliefs and assumptions together. Let that consultant get on the elevator wearing a loin cloth or sporting a large wooden disk in his lower lip. Let the President adopt polygamy and introduce all three of his wives at the Christmas party. Let the CFO fire the corporation's audit firm and abandon the cultural mores we know as accounting rules and tax laws, and the enduring and resilient power of the corporate culture will quickly surface.

There is a *corporate culture*. It has its own language, its own costumes, its own building materials and styles and its own food-getting methods and techniques. It has its own set of shared values, beliefs, and assumptions. This massive and powerful new culture has been spreading throughout the world, drawing millions of people off the cropland into thousands of high-rise office villages and massive factories. Far from having their own unique culture, each corporation is a basic building block of the larger culture. Just as many similar tribes of the Sioux Indians made up a nation, many similar corporations make up an industry such as the automobile, airline or banking industry. Many industries make up what should properly be referred to as the *corporate culture*.

If one accepts the notion that universities are enculturating institutions and that one of their primary functions is to prepare each new generation for taking its place in the larger culture, then course work in accounting, marketing, finance, strategic planning, engineering, manufacturing, and human resources management are delivered for the express purpose of transmitting the knowledge, beliefs, values and shared assumptions that make up the real corporate culture to each new crop of corporate tribesmen and tribes women. Furthermore, universities in America, Europe, Japan, and Saudi Arabia, where cultures vary dramatically, provide course content in business administration that is very similar.

TRIBES

Just as the term *culture* has been garbled and misused by business executives and consultant, there is also a good deal of confusion surrounding the term *tribe*. In her book *Tribal Warfare in Organizations*,[31] Peg Neuhauser asserts that employees in various corporate departments, such as Engineering or Research, because of their different educational backgrounds and affiliations with professional organizations, are vulnerable to interdepartmental conflicts. She calls these conflicts tribal warfare.

---

31. Neuhauser, Peg C., *Tribal Warfare in Organizations* (New York: Harper Collins, 1989).

In a time of multiple tribal affiliations, one can develop serious loyalty to professional tribes such as engineering and accounting organizations. Members may feel some modest loyalty to the American Psychological Association and, indeed, this organization has all the ear markings of a tribe with a dominance hierarchy, income from dues and the sale of journals, a president, employees, and a board of directors. But the dozen or so psychologists in the consulting department of Ernst and Ernst's corporate office in Cleveland do not constitute a tribe. There is no doubt that conflicts between one department and another, within a corporation, occasionally occur; but these are ordinary, run-of-the-mill neighborhood disputes, not tribal warfare.

Where Neuhauser mistakenly calls departments within corporations tribes, Joel Kotkin, quoted earlier, errs in the opposite extreme. He refers to the huge worldwide ethnic and religious diasporas as world tribes. Thus, he confuses tribes with cultures.

In his book *Executive Instinct*,[32] Nigel Nicholson also seems to tap dance when it comes to describing corporations. He calls them "communities" in some places and "clans" in others. His brilliant description of "hardwired" instinctual behavior among executives and his contribution to the new field of Evolutionary Psychology are powerful and persuasive, but he seems unaware that the way humans cluster is also instinctual and that these clusters are the discreet survival units of Homo sapiens. He seems to describe "tribalism" as a kind of disease which must be stamped out.

Corporations are neither communities nor clans. They are evolved tribes. Corporations each have their own tribal histories, their own tribal heroes and legends, as well as their tribal products and services. Each has its own tribal marketing territories and its own unique set of customers, allies and competitors. These corporate tribes are basic building blocks of a new culture — the real corporate culture.

It is clearly possible for executives and consultants to change attitudes, marketing strategies, team effectiveness, the quality and effectiveness of management, products and services, the location, name, size, manufacturing efficiency, and profitability of corporations. It happens every day. In many cases, such changes are essential for survival. These represent changes in tribal

---

32. Nicholson, Nigel, *Executive Instinct Managing the Human Animal in the Information Age* (New York: Crown Publishers, 2000)

customs, methods and techniques. Cultures change slowly. They become ossified with laws, mores, and community standards which require conformity. Cultural changes require generations; they creep at the pace of evolution itself.

Those who understand the real meaning of the term *culture*, which is also the old meaning, used by generations of social scientists, will not succumb to the recent fad which badly misuses the concept. The idea that an outside consultant or a new president can create a new culture for a corporation is preposterous. Anyone who imagines that he is creating new cultures within a corporation is suffering delusions of grandeur.

* * *

Thus far, the archetypal tribal roles within corporations have been described and discussed; and the term "corporate culture" has been more properly defined. In the chapters which follow, the broader ramification of the emergence of this new overarching culture are discussed, particularly the influence this new culture is having on basic institutions that emerged with agriculture.

Chapter Thirteen:
The Relentless Spread of the Corporate Culture

The term *culture* has another definition: the cultivation of living material in prepared nutrient media; also, the product of such cultivation.

If the earth were under the microscope or telescope of some distant alien investigator, the emergence and spread of colonies of buildings would look like a virulent bacteria, like a healthy culture in a petri dish. The first hints of this new earth culture would appear about a hundred years ago in Europe and the United States, but in the past fifty years it would spread dramatically to other continents. The alien would note that the culture was spreading at an increasing rate, and that it was most dense in areas where it began but seemed to flourish everywhere, once it got started.

There were no Southern or Texas or Brooklyn accents in the speech of the first European settlers who arrived in America. As the population increased and spread out, distance alone and the degree of isolation that resulted created some divergence in local speech patterns. Over thousands of years, this same evolutionary process contributed to the emergence of different languages, cultures and religions, perhaps even different races. Barriers like the oceans, mountain ranges, deserts, and climate differences obviously contributed to this divergence.

As populations continued to expand, wars, intermarriage and territorial clashes resulted in a mixing and blending of cultures and languages. The advent of technology and especially the corporate culture has accelerated this blending to the point where divergence is rapidly becoming convergence. Airline pilots from every nation-state must learn English in order to communicate with air traffic controllers. Multinational corporations headquartered in France, Sweden, China, and Malaysia conduct much of their business in English.

When corporate culture is understood in its more accurate definition, it is possible to track how it continues its relentless spread throughout the world. The shared values and mores of the corporate culture as well as its technology are being spread by the most powerful tribal story-tellers ever — television, computers, movies, and music.

In tribal times, the myths and stories were passed down in story telling, dancing and singing. Elaborate rites and costumes were used to get the messages across. Perhaps the court jester is another archetypal role. The standard deck of playing cards is ancient, and it includes two jokers, often used as "wild" cards. They are unpredictable. In some Native American cultures the coyote was regarded as the trickster, the clever spirit that could be good or evil depending on his mood. In the courts of Europe, entertainers could often get away with teasing the King or poking fun at tribal leaders. A serious man could be imprisoned for treason for saying the same things the clown said in jest. Johnny Carson, Dave Letterman and Jay Leno carry on this tradition. They have made fortunes by being irreverent toward politicians. These entertainers were often peripheral to the main activities of the tribe. Traveling gypsies and musicians provided entertainment and carried news and information about what was happening beyond the borders of the kingdom. The Greek thespians told stories of their gods to fascinated audiences. Now, movie and television stars have replaced the tribal gods of Mount Olympus.

Movie stars inspire awe in those who watch them on TV and the big screen. As we watch them play various roles, we get to know them well, every nuance of their personalities — or more disturbing to them, perhaps — the personalities they assume for those roles, which we then mistake for them as individuals. The most convincing and effective corporate chiefs know how to exploit this phenomenon, and consciously play to their audience in order to inspire that awe.

Western movies, television, and pop music now crowd the airwaves and impose their cultural message on the rest of the world. In the propaganda war between West and East, between the US and all others, the power of popular American and British artists is considerable. We hear the same familiar songs by Madonna, the Beatles and Sting in Cairo, Tokyo, Rome, Nairobi, and Rio de

Janeiro. Many songs and movies make political statements and some are potent enough to alter the thinking and opinions of thousands in their target audiences.

Actors, comedians, and musicians have always enjoyed special powers to influence others, but the advent of movies and television has made the few who achieve stardom more powerful than anything that went before. Conan the Barbarian proved this when he became governor of California.

BUSINESS SCHOOL WIZARDS

Some of the most direct transmitters of the new corporate culture are university professors in business schools. Schools like Oxford, Harvard, MIT, University of Chicago and Stanford with strong economics and business curriculums create a "brain drain" in developing countries. Many of the best students, with the greatest promise, enroll to learn about finance, manufacturing methods, marketing, strategic planning, and organization development. Many of them choose to remain in the US and Europe where living standards are further advanced. But many return, and some rise to positions of influence in their nation-states.

Manmoh Singh, the finance minister of India who helped influence India's leaders in economic theory, studied Economics at Cambridge and earned a PhD from Harvard. His colleague, P. Chidambaram, India's Commerce Minister, earned an MBA at Harvard. Both men helped to introduce market-oriented concepts that freed corporations in India from a complex network of state controls and allowed a more rapid participation in the new global economy.

Pedro Aspe of Mexico earned a PhD from MIT. Domingo Cavallo, the Argentine leader, earned a PhD from Harvard, and Ricardo Lagos, elected Chile's President in 2000, earned a PhD in Economics from Duke University. Kwame Nkrumah, Ghana's controversial President, attended the U. of Pennsylvania, and the Polish leader Balcerowicz was educated at St Johns University in New York. Syngman Rhee, South Korea's famous leader, earned a PhD from Princeton University, and in Singapore, Dr. Goh Keng Swee held a PhD from the London School of Economics.[33]

---

33. Mahbubani, Kinshore, *Can Asians Think? Understanding the Divide Between East and West* (Southroyalton, Vermont: Steerforth Press, 2002.)

All of these leaders, and thousands of other students, often the brightest, are absorbing the teachings of a handful of spokesmen for the new corporate message: John Maynard Keynes, Adam Smith, Friedrich von Hayek, and Milton Friedman, among others. From the teachings of these designated heroes, they learn how corporations are to be managed. They study corporate case studies and analyze and evaluate international ventures from approved perspectives. In anthropological terms, they are being enculturated in the technology as well as the mores and values of the corporate culture.

The rate of expansion in the methods, technologies, language, and survival concepts of corporations continues to increase. New MBA and Executive MBA programs are being launched throughout the world; in China, more than 4,000 students have enrolled. *Business Week* reports that there are 21 degree programs run jointly by Chinese and foreign universities, such as Harvard and Fordham, plus 40 more by Chinese universities alone.[34]

ACCOUNTING RULES AS CORPORATE MORES

The notion of hiring outside accountants was not an easy sell two generations ago when the Ernst brothers and the first Arthur Andersen began to promote the benefits of having objective third parties look over and approve the financial dealings of corporations. Now, there is little doubt that the accountants have become permanent elements, and in some cases they do function as the consciences and disciplinarians of the new corporate culture.

In the late 1960s, when Arthur Andersen first attempted to open an accounting office in Moscow, the term "corporate culture" had not yet been invented. It is doubtful that these intrepid accountants realized their concepts and ideas were as culturally potent as those of the early Christian missionaries in places like Samoa and Hawaii. Arthur Andersen gave up on their first attempt precisely because they could not convince Russian businessmen to disclose basic financial data. Even today, European and other corporations doubt the wisdom of allowing outsiders access to sensitive data that would increase their vulnerability to warriors from other tribes, and you won't find many foreign inspectors getting a close look at the books at any U.S. corporations.

---

34. Roberts, Dexter and Li Yan, *China Watch, To Get an MBA is Glorious* (New York: Business Week, April 22, 2002) page 14.

Chapter Thirteen: The Relentless Spread of the Corporate Culture

The concept of annual audits by independent accountants serves as much needed discipline to protect investors, employees, and governments from fraud and tax evasion; however, when the field expanded to include international corporations, it became clear that the major accounting companies are also part of their own national tribes, so that their impartiality comes under question. Each tribe fights to use "our" accountants versus "their" accountants and to apply "our" standards versus "theirs," while seeking to get a peek at the books of the chief competitors in important industries. Most international accounting and consulting firms hire French accountants and consultants to staff their Paris office and Japanese accountants and consultants in Tokyo so that local laws and standards can be understood and followed, but pressures to do things according to home office methods still persist. Furthermore, it has lately become more obvious that even on a domestic level the idea of third-party auditing accountability does not guarantee objectivity. The scandals at Enron and Arthur Andersen show that partners in some major accounting firms have, in fact, lost their third party objectivity and become part of their corporate clients' tribes.

Bankers have the reputation of being solid, honest, responsible members of their communities. Ordinary citizens trust their local banks to hold their money, feeling it is safer there than under the mattress. But every once in awhile a group of federal or state auditors arrive, unannounced. They examine the bank's loan and investment portfolios, count the cash, and review a long list of management practices. Most of the time, they find the bank is "clean." But occasionally they discover that bankers have been making loans to themselves or their friends at ridiculously low rates of interest. Sometimes they discover too many bad loans where customers have fallen so far behind that repayment is unlikely. They may discover that the President is paying himself, his son, or his wife huge salaries. Disclosing these problems could easily cause a run on the bank. Instead, the auditors install a "work out" plan. The bank's leaders are required to comply with corrective measures under more careful supervision and more frequent audits. When problems are too serious to correct, the owners can lose their charter and the bank quietly sold to others.

In the 1970s, after a period of lax controls, widespread fraud was discovered in the U.S. Savings and Loan industry. Many S&L executives were using their depositor's money for highly speculative real estate loans or for their own huge salaries, expensive company cars and apartments. It took many years and billions of taxpayer dollars to bail out the industry.

The lessons are clear. Business men, like all men, are greedy. Their effort to circumvent accounting rules and laws are often ingenious. To achieve a level of trust that is sufficient to attract investors, independent third party audits continue to be essential.

Some analysts believe that as the U.S. initiated reforms following scandals, such as the implosion at Enron and the more recent departure of Richard Grasso, head of the New York Stock Exchange, following disclosure of his $140 million compensation package, others around the globe are quietly following suit. Eric Pfanner, writing for the International Herald Tribune, points out that improving corporate governance is a refrain now heard across most developed countries and that even countries like Macedonia and Pakistan, hardly hubs of multinational business, are trying to assure the independence of accountants, empowering shareholders, and increasing the transparency of financial reporting. Pfanner believes these seemingly paradoxical reactions reflect the power of globalized financial markets.[35] They also reflect the continued expansion of the mores of the corporate culture.

At the same time many international businessmen see today's so-called security concerns as an outright attempt to have the American accounting firms gain access to non-American companies, including those in western Europe, under the pretext that the US requires higher standards of accounting. They are, in fact, less rigorous than European standards, according to the *International Herald Tribune*. However, to be listed in US stock markets, such firms are now required to submit to US-style audits and to disclose information that their own national governments do not consider a matter of public record.

Following basic accounting rules, accurately disclosing information on sales, operating expenses, profits and losses have become such pillars of the corporate culture that when errors and fraud are discovered, stock prices tumble, great fortunes are lost, and great corporations disintegrate. Sadly, the great Arthur Anderson, with its many thousands of bright, honest, hard working professionals, was shocked to discover that the poor judgment of a few partners could bring such a great firm to its knees.

Even though top executives of major banks complained loudly in the late 1970s when laws were passed that required full disclosure of their compen-

---

35. Pfanner, Eric *A new way of doing business. Scandals lead to reform in the U.S., and others quietly follow* (International Harold Tribune, September 23, 2003).

sation, including salaries, bonuses and stock options, they eventually complied. Now, anyone can get copies of their corporate SEC filings and with a little digging and a knowledge of how stock options and bonus plans work, can figure out how much top executives are paid. The information is usually shocking, especially to hourly wage-earning employees. Major corporate executives can amass vast fortunes, especially if they develop a successful track record of growing the business — which is to say, driving the value of the stock up.

GLOBALIZATION

In *The Commanding Heights*,[36] Daniel Yergin and Joseph Stanislaw provide a wonderfully documented account of the impact of market focused economic policies, with its international finance, management science, technology, and global economic theories, on nation-states throughout the world over the past fifty years. They show, "Why and how the shift from an era in which the 'state' — national governments — sought to seize and exercise control over their economies to an era in which the ideas of competition, openness, privatization, and deregulation have captured world economic thinking."

In one country after another, the tidal wave of economic reforms have been undertaken to allow corporations more freedom from nation-state controls and restrictions. Trade barriers have come down. Foreign trade and investment have increased. Massive privatization has occurred in countries that had been thoroughly controlled by a dominant government. Many of the countries experienced periods of rapid growth after initiating reforms in their policies, reducing government controls, and allowing their companies the independence needed to become more market focused. Russia and China, who were opposed to anything "capitalistic," have rationalized their economic policies in a way that allows them to participate in the new world economy.

"All around the globe, socialists are embracing capitalism, governments are selling off companies they had previously nationalized, and countries are seeking to entice back multinational corporations they had expelled just two decades earlier."[37]

---

36. Yergan, Daniel and Joseph Stanislaw, *The Commanding Heights — The Battle for the World Economy* (New York: Simon & Schuster, 1998).
37. Op. cit.

The term "globalization" seemed like an abstract concept only a few years ago. Yergin and Stanislaw described it this way:

> Globalization is a move to a more connected world in which barriers and borders of many kinds — from the Iron Curtain to corporate identity to government control of airwaves — are coming down, felled both by technological change, especially technologies that bring down the costs of transportation and communication, and by ideas and policies that bring down the barriers to the movement of people, goods, and information.[38]

Today, more than $1.5 trillion dollars flies across nation-state borders on credit card purchases, wire transfers, currency and security trades *every day*. The worldwide communications network has shrunk the earth permanently.

In *The Lexus and the Olive Tree*, Thomas L. Friedman asserts that globalization, with its concepts of free market capitalism, has replaced the Cold War as the defining international system.

> It is the inexorable integration of markets, nation-states and technologies to a degree never witnessed before in a way that is enabling individuals, corporations and nation-states to reach around the world farther, faster, deeper, and cheaper than ever before, and in a way that is enabling the world to reach into individuals, corporations and nation-states farther faster, and deeper than ever before.[39]

Friedman explains that adopting the rules and methods of free market capitalism is like putting on what he calls a "golden straight jacket." Golden, because it generates wealth in countries that choose to participate. A straight jacket, because the required rules of accounting and transparency restrict and limit behavior and those who break the rules can suffer severe economic consequences.

In this respect, in fact, all cultures are a kind of straight jacket. They control what members eat and wear, what gods they worship, who they can marry, what language they speak, even how they think and solve problems. Friedman's "golden straight jacket" is another way of describing the corporate culture.

---

38. Op. cit., page 383
39. Friedman, Thomas L., *The Lexus and the Olive Tree* (New York: Anchor Books, 2000).

Chapter Thirteen: The Relentless Spread of the Corporate Culture

Globalization seems to have its own momentum, outpacing the imagination and understanding of the worlds most learned economists. On July 2, 1997, the collapse of the Thai *baht* did not arouse much concern among world class economists — at first. But it set off the Asian contagion that swept its way across emerging markets with a fury that caused a good deal of panic among international investors. It hit Korea, then Russia, then Brazil. When it began to affect US markets, it left world economic leaders shaken and demonstrated that any control they believed they had was less complete than they had thought; in fact, their control was perhaps nothing more than an arrogant illusion.

Everyone acknowledges that stock markets are influenced by such factors as investor confidence and mob psychology, but as the scale and scope of financial markets move to a global stage, economist realize they have a huge, dangerous and unpredictable tiger by the tail.

In the United States, no one predicted how quickly the national debt would grow in the Nixon and Reagan years, nor did they forecast how quickly it would melt away when the sustained period of economic growth of the 90s generated such enormous increases in tax revenues. Now, of course, the debt is coming back even faster than it evaporated.

The intricate growth of the global economy seems to have its own momentum and it is not fully understood or controlled by the IMF, the World Bank, the Federal Reserve or the NYSE. The corporate culture has already soaked into the fabric of the entire world's economic policies, and the rate at which it is spreading continues to accelerate. The process has not always been a smooth one.

The rules and mores of the corporate culture have been evolving steadily, and it is unreasonable to expect nations with diverse cultural histories to adopt them overnight. Indeed, they cannot, since many aspects are intertwined with cultural and historical factors. In this respect, the West views the IMF and the World Bank both as Santa Claus and the drill sergeant — while developing countries wonder whether they are being propelled along the road to ruin by false prophets. To the extent that the rules are set by one tribe or one alliance of tribes, those tribes on the "outside" have a difficult path forward.

The scandal associated with the Salt Lake City Olympics and the subsequent expulsion of IOC committee members who took bribes is another example of how the values of the corporate culture are being enforced. Bribes are taboo.

As with other cultures, the rules and mores of the corporate culture have become codified into laws. After only a few generations, there are already libraries filled with tax laws, labor laws, securities laws, pollution, health, safety, patent and employment laws. The most developed countries lead the way in creating and enforcing these emerging corporate mores. For example, there are new laws currently being developed in the US that will protect employee retirement plans from the greed of top executives. In time, these laws may also become part of the worldwide corporate culture.

The spread of corporations throughout the earth is dramatic. There are now 60,000 multinational corporations and one in seven US manufacturing employees works for a foreign company. The rules they employ to govern things like buying, selling, and disclosure of financial information, is evidence of a new culture. It should properly be referred to as *The Corporate Culture*. Individual corporations do have their own unique tribal customs, but they do not have separate or distinct cultures. In fact, if and when they depart from the rules and mores of the larger corporate culture, outside pressures to conform emerge and eventually prevail.

THE NEW CORPORATE LOYALTY

As the new corporate culture is disseminated throughout the world, will it alleviate widespread poverty and reduce the incidence of bloody war? The jury is still out, but the changes taking place may offer a new chance at a better future.

In the meantime, some longstanding tribal values are changing. One of these is loyalty.

Earlier tribal adaptations were concrete, in the sense that all the tribe members could actually see and touch all the people and property. But as tribes got larger and more scattered tribes became what Benedict Anderson referred to as "imagined communities".[40] It soon became physically impossible for a Pope to visit all the churches and cathedrals in his realm, let alone meet all those who called themselves Catholics. In today's large corporations only a handful of top executives see or touch the entire corporation. Their plants and offices are often scattered all over the face of the earth. Inviting *all* the employees to gather in one

---

40. Anderson, Benedict *Imagined Communities: Reflections on the Origin and Spread of Nationalism* (London and New York: Verso, 1991).

Chapter Thirteen: The Relentless Spread of the Corporate Culture

place for a meeting is practically impossible. A diligent CEO may travel to most of the major plants and offices of a newly acquired company but even these senior officers often control people and properties that they never actually meet and see. Employees, investors, stockholders, competitors; even board members and executives can only imagine the full extent of their employees and corporate holdings. Instead they see columns of financial data as well as a few photographs and descriptive paragraphs in the annual report. The big picture, the complete corporate entity, only exists in their imagination. No wonder the old values of loyalty have become diluted.

In hunting and gathering and agricultural societies, loyalty was often a life-and-death proposition. Losing a battle often meant death to the adult males and slavery for their wives and children. Fighting fiercely, to the death when necessary, is seen as heroism in all agricultural societies. War veterans are honored everywhere with monuments and national holidays.

The loyalties that form among soldiers during battle are among the strongest known to man. However, in the new corporate tribes, that kind of loyalty is neither generated nor expected.

Not only do corporate tribes require less loyalty from employees, they offer less loyalty to them. Major corporations buy and sell companies almost continually and relatively little concern is given to those employees who will be getting a new corporate owner. There is little evidence that corporations feel guilty when they fire large groups of employees, and massive layoffs and downsizing are commonplace. Some corporations must downsize in order to survive. Many others that are in little or no danger of failure do it simply to improve profits.

Nevertheless, corporations work hard to encourage loyalty and commitment from employees, of course with mixed results. Just as the corporations do not hesitate to jettison employees, workers and executives alike are quite ready to quit and join a competitor at the first opportunity. Most employees, including executives, work with several corporations during their careers. The individual who stays with one company through an entire career is the exception rather than the rule. All prior tribal affiliations, to one's nation-state, religion, or hunting and gathering tribe, were life-and-death, cradle-to-grave commitments. The multiple tribal affiliations of modern men and women tend to dilute loyalty.

When Coca Cola opened its stock purchase and stock option programs to all of its employees, worldwide, workers became financially as well as emotionally concerned with their company's continued growth and prosperity. They naturally feel a sense of loyalty to Coca Cola, especially when much of their wealth and retirement security depends on the company's continued prosperity. Coca Cola clearly benefits from this loyalty. But unlike nation-states, Coca Cola would not dream of asking their employees to die or kill for the company. No employee of Coca Cola expects to have to prove his or her loyalty to the corporation by physically attacking Pepsi employees. Coke employees have to be careful not to order a Pepsi when having lunch with the boss, but in terms of loyalty, corporations require far less than nation-states.

At one point in the 1990s, Philips, the huge multinational corporation from the Netherlands primarily known for its electronics products, owned more than 800 separate companies scattered all over the face of the earth, each with its own products, services, logos, employee groups, and management teams. For an individual Philips employee working in China, France, or Singapore, the corporate headquarters in Eindhoven was an abstract figment of their imagination, a kind of mother tribe that provided money and resources, and occasional management talent. Few of the thousands of Philips employees had a clear grasp of the entire tribe, beyond what they read about in the annual report. They focused on their own work groups, their own products and customers. They developed loyalty to their immediate leaders and co-workers.

When Philips began to "sell off the bleeders" to improve its return on investment for shareholders. Dozens of weak and marginally performing companies went to new owners. For the vast majority of individual employees, getting new ownership was not a traumatic event — not at all like when Germany occupied France! Employees saw some strangers in suits come to visit the company. Then news arrived that the company had been sold; but this was not really a surprise, since most employees knew their performance, in terms of profitability, was not meeting Philips' standards. A new General Manager and Controller arrived. All the employees were assembled to watch a taped message sent out by the CEO of the acquiring company. A new name went up over the door, new business cards were issued, new stationery was printed and new packages arrived to wrap the products in. The day-to-day activities of most employees continued without disruption. Within a few weeks, employee loyalty was successfully refocused on the new corporation.

Some executives survive a change of ownership year after year. Those who are most secure tend to be those who succeed, despite the turmoil, to consis-

Chapter Thirteen: The Relentless Spread of the Corporate Culture

tently reach or exceed their profit targets. Softer, subjectively measured goals may not impress the incoming management team; but there are measurable performance goals, and even if the results are assessed by someone different each time around, the numbers speak for themselves. This kind of success also makes it likely that the team of experienced employees will also be kept intact through the succession of owners.

In corporate tribes, the issue of loyalty is also diluted by the division between employees and shareholders. Top executive teams are often more driven by the need to serve key stockholders than by their loyalty to employees. Hundreds of employees, entire sub-tribes, can be dumped if the result will increase the value of the stock. When top executives and board members are major stockholders, as is often the case, loyalty to employee groups becomes a distant second or third place consideration.

One form of corporate loyalty is the commitment the major owners and stockholders, whose fortunes are at risk, have to each other and to the business venture. Their motivations are selfish — to increase their own wealth.

Of course, major corporate decisions can hardly be made out of loyalty to *all* stockholders. When a small investor buys stock in a company, he, too, does it for selfish financial motives. As a rule, he does not know any of the executives who run the company, never attends stockholder meetings, or vote the proxies that come in the mail. He feels no sense of loyalty to the company or its employees, and he does not expect the company he invests in to be more loyal to him than it is to its own employees. Small investors are essentially hitchhikers, gambling on the ideas, capabilities, and decisions of a handful of major investors and top executive leaders.

Among top level executives, especially those who have been betrayed in political maneuvering, loyalty is still highly valued. They usually feel a keen sense of betrayal and disappointment when a talented subordinate leaves to join another company. Most effective leaders develop an entourage of loyal followers who help them succeed and ride their coattails as they advance. At top levels, some executives take key members of their entourage with them when they change companies. Knowing this, the ambitious middle manager must be careful in choosing a boss. When an executive gets squeezed out during the competition for a top job, all their nearest subordinates may find their days numbered, too. Conversely, if their boss gets promoted to CEO, they may become a VP.

A loyal manager knows when and where to pledge his or her allegiance, and when it is done with sincerity it can be enormously effective.

> "I just want you to know that you have my total allegiance. If you need anything, if I can help you or our team succeed in any way, just ask."

A cluster of talented, hard-working executives who are loyal to the boss and to each other can help protect each other's careers. Being able to trust team members allows everyone to focus on other challenges. Knowing what the corporation expects from them, they know how to defend their positions and promote themselves. This kind of loyalty requires that when a team member is criticized in your presence (by someone outside the team), you stoutly defend him or her. Let your loyalty shine.

Corporations measure loyalty not only by the results of a group's labor, but also by the "soft" or non-measurable displays of loyalty, like an employee's defense of the company's interest in the presence of employees of other companies. Astute employees know how to use to their advantage this need for tribal display and they go to considerable lengths to demonstrate their commitment, from wearing the company golf shirt to speaking at conferences and meetings. They become the best propagandists for the company.

Similarly, some clever managers band together to advance their careers. Consciously or unconsciously, they may follow the rule that "one hand washes the other." When any attempt at self promotion would be seen as boasting, they boost each other, instead. Every time one of their names surfaces in corporate meetings or informal discussion around the coffee machine, they say something positive: "He's a great salesman," or "Wow, what a hard worker." Doing favors and returning favors, thy advance their informal little sub-tribe.

Stock ownership for hourly employees, stock options for management, and the many corporate programs which encourage employees to become owners represent powerful methods by which the corporation generates loyalty. Even though the class structures of the agricultural era, landowners vs. serfs and sharecroppers, still exist in the blue collar vs. management and hourly vs. salaried policies of corporations, employees who own a bit of stock feel that they have broken through this ancient barrier.

In its early years, Microsoft paid employees partially in stock. (Perhaps they still do.) Salaries were kept at or below competitive levels. This not only reduced their operating expenses, it also built loyalty. Employees became

Chapter Thirteen: The Relentless Spread of the Corporate Culture

invested in the company's future. The result has been many millionaires. Dozens of Microsoft's managers and executives who are so wealthy they can hardly spend all of their money in their lifetime still show up for work everyday. The financial incentive is no longer there, but the loyalty remains.

Employees become more valuable when they understand the corporation's products, customers, and daily business challenges and it becomes costly when corporations lose experienced employees. It is also expensive to attract experienced people from competitors. Programs are put in place to consciously create and enhance employee loyalty. Some give shirts and caps with corporate logos to employees at meetings and conferences. Corporate flags, colors, mottos, and anthems are becoming more common. Some corporations sponsor shared vacations for employees, and management conferences in exotic locations, often including spouses. Employee recognition sessions are common where awards or pins are given for those who reach ten or twenty year anniversaries. A key objective of these shared vacations and experiences is to encourage camaraderie and esprit de corps within the team.

Corporate-sponsored sports teams such as soccer, softball, and volleyball are intended to have a similar effect, as are hobby groups and book clubs. Essentially, any activity which captures the discretionary time of employees under a corporate banner tends to inhibit or foreclose competing loyalties. Employees who work for big corporations in small towns are more likely to establish friendships and spend evenings and weekends with other employees than those in large urban centers. This too, encourages loyalty.

In case these lures are not sufficient to keep everyone on the reservation, non-compete contracts, loyalty oaths and golden handcuff compensation packages close the lock.

JOB HOPPERS AND DOWNSIZERS

Since loyalty means so little to so many, many executives have turned job-hopping into an art. Just after bonuses and raises are paid by one company they move to the next. These job hoppers can get to top level positions faster as they turn their own disloyalty for the company into disloyalty for their employees by firing subordinates and arranging massive lay offs. But, corporate tribes have become far more fluid and adaptable than all prior human tribes. Companies can be acquired and divested easily, to fit the evolving vision and growth plans of a few corporate leaders. The traditional concept of loyalty has become less urgent in corporate tribes.

Just as modern men and women have multiple tribal affiliations, they also have multiple loyalties. Most have strong attachments to their religions and their alma mater. Many become fiercely loyal to the nearest professional football, basketball or hockey team, so much so that they paint their faces, don strange costumes at games and wear the team's colors and logo. When their nation-state gets involved in a war, many are willing to enlist or submit to the draft in the belief that whatever they are told is a threat to their country is a threat worth sacrificing for. Like the barons, serfs and peons of an earlier time, they leave their corporations to join the army or navy.

Loyalty to one's religion and nation-state are still powerful; nonetheless, for the past half a century, the demand for loyalty to the corporation has a growing impact on the lives of millions of employees. In their competition to attract talented and capable employees, those corporations that can build and enhance loyalty have a powerful edge over those who struggle with labor disputes and must continually hire and train new employees to replace experienced ones who leave.

Corporate Greed

Average employees rarely gets a view of life at the top, but when they do, it makes an impact. When one gets invited to meet such a retired executive, say, a corporate board member, at his estate, the chauffeur drives him up a road lined with sparkling white fences. Horses frisk in the fields, beautiful, sleek black and sorrel mares, and a magnificent coal black stallion in a field of his own. A gigantic cobblestone courtyard with a fountain and banks of flowers gives way to a magnificent mansion, a modern granite compound with enormous picture windows. A full-size racetrack and several large white buildings give the appearance of an exclusive country resort.

The owner usually is articulate and has strong opinions.

After the interview, the man invites his guest over to the track where they sit in a luxury box, order drinks from another uniformed servant and watches some attractive girls exercise elegant race horses — the kind of experience one

Chapter Thirteen: The Relentless Spread of the Corporate Culture

imagines would be offered to some Arabian prince who had dropped in to buy horses or arrange stud services. All beautiful and elegant.

When the guest leaves, a chauffeur drives him back to the airport away from a world he had seen glimpses of — only in movies. Americans still think this is only in the movies, when in fact it is the quintessential reality of class society, everywhere.

It can be similarly shocking to visit Versailles, the Hearst castle in California, the Hidden City in Beijing, and the royal palace compound in Bangkok. The $16.8 million New York apartment of Dennis Kozlowski, Tyco's ex-CEO, is every bit as shocking as the Palace at Versailles.

When Clarence Darrow, the famous lawyer in the Scopes trial who defended the teaching of evolution in the classroom, spoke to the inmates of Chicago's infamous Cook County jail, he posed an analogy something like the following:

If mankind were to discover a new continent, like Australia, and one thousand families, each with $20,000, were sent there to colonize it, there would be no crime. But in ten or twenty years, a few families would amass hundreds of thousands of dollars and large estates while others would have very little. Crime would emerge as those with very little attempted to survive. The wealthy families would then make laws and hire sheriffs and policemen to protect their property and build jails and prisons to lock up those who broke those laws. To Darrow, crime was a response to a basic element of unfairness in man's natural abilities to amass wealth.

Of course, corporations did not invent greed. Leaders have lived in opulent splendor, while their citizens lived in poverty, since the beginnings of civilization. Even today, as the average CEO in the US earns 500 times more than the average worker (663 times more than the minimum wage), the US compensation picture resembles the old feudal system to a dismaying degree.

There is no doubt that the earliest factories were horrible, dehumanizing places. Owners of the earliest industries created corporate serfdoms and did everything they could to keep workers in a state of economic slavery. Karl Marx was deeply disturbed by working conditions in the Lancashire manufacturing districts where children were tied to their work benches and flogged when they failed to meet their quotas. Communism had tremendous appeal to millions of exploited workers whose hatred of the privileged bourgeoisie fueled revolutions. Yet the corporations continue to this day to exploit the toiling masses with low wages and working conditions that are against the law in the books in their own countries.

However, as corporations and their workers have evolved over several generations and the greedy excesses and cruelties of owners have been exposed, laws have been created that have curbed, and modified these excesses. Many of the departments of the US government such as OSHA, the SEC, the FDA, the Comptroller of the Currency, and Department of Labor exist for the sole purpose of controlling and regulating various form of corporate greed.

In this environment and despite harsh opposition from the corporate barons, the labor movement in industrialized nations of Europe and the United States did make tremendous progress in winning higher wages and improved working conditions for millions of corporate employees. The struggle has not been easy and it still continues.

Corporate Democracy

The notion of one share — one vote is a deeply embedded feature of the corporate culture. Big shareholders, particularly the majority shareholder, make all the major decisions. In this respect, major shareholders parallel landowners of the agricultural era. If most of the employees vote to paint the lunch room green, and the majority shareholder wants it to be pink, it will be pink.

The result is that a great many corporations are run by dictators and some of them, especially in family-owned corporations, act as though God anointed them.

When an employee becomes a shareholder, he or she gets access to annual reports and other more or less confidential information. When the employees' financial assets, as well as their incomes, are tied to their companies, they tend to see things differently than the employee who owns no stock. They can attend stockholder meetings and begin to feel they are part of an elite sub-group within the tribe.

Many corporations, recognizing the advantage of making more employees stockholders, have created program that offer substantial discounts for employees who wish to purchase shares. Others have invested chunks of the employee's retirement funds in company stock or offered lucrative stock options to key managers.

Chapter Thirteen: The Relentless Spread of the Corporate Culture

When these plans were new, they were promoted as ways to motivate employees and align employee efforts to those of the leaders. Benefits to the company include being able to pay (at least in part) with paper instead of cash, being able to boast about the number of outstanding shares and value (on a short-term basis), and spreading the risk in case business does not go well. As proven by a number of scandals, too often such schemes end up defrauding the employees, who find themselves out of work and stripped of their deferred payment, and retirement funds, as well. Even short of such disaster, stock options can easily go "under water." When the value of the stock falls below the option price and employee stockholders see their financial resources and retirement benefits deteriorate, they can become angry and critical of their leaders. When employees begin to suspect that the company is paying them with stock rather than cash only in order to manipulate share price or to evade responsibility for retirement funding, motivation drops even faster.

United Airlines became the first major employee-owned air carrier in the US. Many predicted smoother relationships with unions, increased motivation and productivity from employees and improved levels of customer service; but these admirable goals seem not to have materialized, nor did they save the company from bankruptcy.

When companies like Enron can fool their accountants and experienced members of their own board, typical employees have little hope of understanding what shenanigans their leaders employ. The life savings of hard-working employees can be destroyed in each such incident. And the hundreds of thousands of men in prison for stealing a car or a TV set must wonder how executive thieves who steal millions can get away without being punished.

THE TRIBELESS REMAINDER

As the mighty ship of corporate culture plows forward, not everyone can manage to get on board or stay on board. In its wake we see the disintegration of small farming towns, a fracturing of extended families, homeless people sleeping in cardboard boxes, huge welfare costs and prisons bursting at the seams. In industrialized nations, every large city must deal with the immense social problems of those who cannot get or hold a job. Indeed, many intelligent people resist the notion of signing on to the corporate culture, and resent the pressure to be part of such an artificial tribe.

Of course, corporations do all they can to screen out those with poor educational achievement. Professional employment agencies further screen out anyone who doesn't fit the mold. The end result is that most corporations are successful in developing conformist employees, even if they are otherwise capable, intelligent, well-educated, and productive. Many of those who are more individualistic find careers in small businesses.

One offshoot of the obfuscation concerning corporate discriminatory employment is the refusal to acknowledge publicly its employment practices, based on the normal curve in the area of intelligence. In Lake Wobegone, Garrison Keillor's fictional small town at the edge of the prairie — a model of "corporate" life — "all the men are strong, all the women are good looking and all the children are above average." No parents want to accept that their child is not above average, especially where intelligence is concerned. It is much less painful to believe that their child has Dyslexia, Attention Deficit Disorder, hyperactivity, autism, or a learning disability. Of course, many children with good intellectual capabilities do have these disorders; but many others are simply not very smart. It has become politically unpopular to believe that not all children are above average and one has to be reminded that for every child with an IQ of 120 (the average for those in college), there is another child on the other side of the "normal" curve with an IQ of 80. By definition, there are as many people with IQs below 80 as there with IQs above 120.

In fact, trends in corporate employment prove that they know very well what they are looking for and the opportunity is not equal in any sense. Good-looking people get cushy jobs in the front office; those with lower IQs and less impressive appearances sweep the floors, in the back. And it seems as though it "just happens" that way. Meanwhile, the unemployed, an army of reserves, is a corporate invention that keeps pressure and discipline on the rank and file.

In a society where "What's good for GM is good for America," and as a direct result of corporate employment policies, the society as a whole ends up not directing enough attention at those with below average intelligence. Society focuses on preparing children for joining the hunting and gathering activities of corporate tribes. Those who have difficulty in school and often drop out. Those unable to read, make change at the cash register, or work with computers have a hard time finding jobs. Without at least a high school education, few of them find careers with corporations.

Chapter Thirteen: The Relentless Spread of the Corporate Culture

In their book *The Bell Curve — Intelligence and Class Structure in American Life*, Herrnstein and Murray show how low intelligence contributes to poverty, unemployment, welfare dependency, illegitimacy, and crime in the United States. For example, their research has shown that, "more than nine out of ten men who described themselves as too disabled to work were in the bottom quarter of the IQ distribution." Among white chronic welfare recipients, only 4% had degrees beyond high school; 38% had less than a high school diploma. "Among the most firmly established facts about criminal offenders is that their distribution of IQ scores differs from that of the population at large. Taking the scientific literature as a whole, criminal offenders have average IQs of about 92, eight points below the mean."[41]

In their admirably thorough review of scientific literature, Herrnstein and Murray also show that divorce rates are higher in people with lower intelligence, they are not as good in the area of parenting and their families are less stable.

Some authorities believe that 80% of the social problems in major cities come from the lowest 20% in terms of IQ. Yet there are jobs for low IQ citizens that provide dignity, adequate wages and solid contributions to society — just not enough of them, and not enough programs to identify and train people to fill them.

In Singapore, there are no homeless men sleeping in doorways. Those who fall through the cracks are assigned to keep a section of street in the city clean. They are given a small room and enough pay to buy food and basic supplies. One result is that Singapore is one of the cleanest large cities in the world.

As technology advances and the requirement for job knowledge increases the years of education required clearly increase. One or two generations ago, young men and women married earlier and joined the adult work force at a much younger age. Today, many professional careers require four to six years of graduate school beyond the bachelor's degree and those not blessed with above average intelligence have no chance.

Herrnstein and Murray describe the emergence of a new class which they call the "cognitive elite." These bright, well educated, well employed individuals find jobs with corporations, live in affluent suburbs and are becoming increasingly insulated and isolated from the social problems of the inner city. They

---

41. Herrnstein, R. and Murray, C., *The Bell Curve — Intelligence and Class Structure in American Life* (New York: Free Press, 1994). Page 155 and 199.

predict a deteriorating quality of life for people at the bottom end of the cognitive ability distribution.

In a way, a class structure that replaces aristocratic families with those who are most intelligent may be a good thing. It releases talent and provides opportunity for advancement based on merit for individuals who in earlier times would have been blocked by tradition. On the other hand, being born into a wealthy aristocratic family and being born with high intelligence are both matters of luck. So, too, being born in poverty and being born with low intelligence are both matters of bad luck.

WHERE IS GRANDPA?

Corporate employees have to go where the company sends them. They are expected to fall into line when the caravan sets off; the nomadic lifestyle is back — especially at management levels. They frequently pull up stakes and move to some new city in order to advance their careers. The result is a fracturing of family, church and community ties, leaving such people more dependent and more closely tied to the only tribe they have left: the corporation.

The nomadic nature of corporate careers as well as high divorce rates are separating millions of modern children from their fathers, grandparents, uncles, aunts and cousins. Small towns, another form of tribes, also provide rich tapestries of relationships, complex networks of friendships and acquaintances that contribute to the socialization of young people. Everyone knows everyone else's business in small towns. The comfort these relationships provide is no longer available when families relocate every few years.

In the big cities of the corporate culture, everyone knows that you can live for years in a high rise apartment and never get to know the people across the hall. More and more, the same applies to the modern housing developments which warehouse the working class across the nation — whether in condominiums or suburban houses. We spend far more time with TV personalities than with neighbors. Where our relationships with family and village friends are deteriorating, television is providing a new electronic village. Walter Cronkite, Tom Brokaw, and Daniel Shore have become our village elders. Katie Couric has become the village sweetheart and when her husband died, we all grieved with her and wanted to comfort her. Dave Letterman and Jay Leno are our zany old friends, our village jesters.

Chapter Thirteen: The Relentless Spread of the Corporate Culture

In earlier tribal adaptations, individuals grew up surrounded by their extended family. In Samoa, grandparents and young girls played a major role in child rearing, allowing young mothers an active social life. The large tribal clusters of hunting and gathering tribes shrank when families dispersed across broad cultivated farmlands, and the move from farms to the cities has shrunk them again.

Whether they live in apartments or individual houses, families often become isolated. Each person may work for a different corporation, in a different industry; they have fewer shared interests with the others living nearby. If they work together, they may be rivals or feel that it is safer to keep their personal lives separate from the dynamics of the workplace. Without the large cast of characters provided by the tribe or the extended family, couples must rely on each other for everything. This single fragile relationship may be overloaded as modern men and women look to their spouses for all the entertainment, pleasure, support and guidance that used to be provided by an entire village. No wonder so many feel lonely and spend so much time watching the soap operas of the TV village. No wonder almost half of all marriages in industrialized countries end in divorce. And, of course, divorce results in an additional fracturing into even smaller clusters.

Now, as the mass migration from small farm towns to the factories and offices of corporate tribes continues, one sees buildings in rural towns boarded up and empty dusty streets. As Paul Simon lamented, there is "nothing but the dead and dying in my hometown." The vulnerability of small farms and small farm towns in America resulting from the rapid emergence of the corporate culture, and the immense social problems that have arisen in large cities in Europe and the United States, are clearly being repeated in other parts of the world. In Caracas, Buenos Aires, Mexico City, Bangkok and Rio de Janeiro, huge pockets of poverty have emerged as poor families with limited job skills have moved to the big cities to search for jobs.

Problems of crime, divorce, industrial diseases, pollution of the air and the oceans, global warming and depletion of natural resources have all been unintended results of the rapid emergence of the corporate culture. All of these issues are likely to get worse unless nation-states and their corporate tribes radically change their nature.

Individual corporations do not have their own separate cultures. They have their own tribal customs, but the real corporate culture encompasses all modern corporations, their common practices such as accounting and tax rules, as well as their own language, costumes and building materials.

The real corporate culture is spreading rapidly throughout all the cultures on earth via movies, television, music and international travel as well as by business schools in Europe and America. In just the past ten years, a complex network of trade relationships driven by multi-billion dollar multinational corporations has turned globalization from an abstract theory into a reality.

Those at the centers of power always enjoyed a double advantage by taking advantage of their own employees and working people, and those of the outlying districts as well — in this case, the Third World. The other side of the coin is that the working poor of the Third World suffer a double-whammy, being taken advantage of by their own local corporate minions and the larger corporate mandarins from Headquarters, too.

The mass migration from farms to cities that marks the rise of the corporate culture has caused many unintended problems and social disruptions, including a disintegration of the extended family, increased rates of divorce, increased crime rates and welfare dependency, particularly with those who are unable to get adequate education and employment due to low intelligence. These trends are likely to amplify, if left unaddressed.

PART THREE

NATION-STATES AND MULTINATIONAL CORPORATIONS AS WORLD TRIBES

Chapter Fourteen:
Nation-States as Tribes

From the beginnings of agriculture until the time of our grandfathers, the largest human clusters have been nation-states. Even though they are far larger than the human clusters we tend to think of as tribes, these nation-states do organize and function like all other human clusters. Every nation-state has its hunter/warriors. Nation-state armies are larger than bands of tribal warriors and they are better equipped, trained and organized. They are mostly made up of full-time soldiers rather than part-time hunters. On the many occasions in history where nation-state armies clashed with tribal warriors from hunting and gathering societies, the warriors usually lost. (Custer's defeat at the Little Bighorn was a rare exception.)

The same principles of organization, size, and full time vs. part time are characteristic of how each of the tribal archetypes developed as nation-states emerged. Gatherers became full-time tax collectors, nurses, schoolteachers, innkeepers, entertainers, nannies, servants, gardeners, cooks, ladies in waiting, and other kinds of service providers.

As in other forms of evolution, new more specialized, complex and differentiated roles emerged.

Each nation-state has its wizards, court priests, sages, seers, healers, and religious leaders. The power and influence of these men and women of knowledge varies substantially. They create and control ceremonies including coronations, marriages, baptisms, funerals, and various priesthood initiations. In many cases, such wizards have been able to completely tie up the political alpha with traditions, pomp and ceremony to a degree that his or her power was neutralized. In several civilizations, churches became larger and more powerful than nation-states, or encompassed more than one nation-state. The wizards who led them became powerful political leaders.

Every nation-state had one or more councils of elders. Courts, senates, parliaments, cabinets, dumas and other clusters of mature and elderly citizen leaders are standard features of nation-state tribes, just as they were with earlier tribal mutations.

Each nation-state had its Alpha who became the center of tribal attention and was worshiped and feared with irrational and obsessive zeal. Each nation-state still tracks its history as a succession of alphas and changes in alpha, either by election, assassination, or natural death, mark the beginnings of new chapters in that nations history.

Each nation-state provides multiple arenas where struggles for dominance are played out allowing the strongest, most intelligent and craftiest to gain and use power.

These agricultural nation-states divided the physical geography of the earth into patches. Their armies were used to protect a patch of territory or to enlarge it by expanding into new territories. Oceans, mountain ranges and rivers provided natural barriers and often became national borders. Over the centuries, smaller nation-states were conquered and absorbed by larger ones until most encompassed clusters and combinations of diverse cultures, religions and languages. The dominant clans and families who rose to power tended to spread their language and culture throughout their kingdoms and suppress competing belief systems.

The USA as a Tribe

The United States was modeled on the tribe, from the very beginning, and still is. It has a Chief and many sub chiefs, such as the Vice President, Secretary of Defense, Secretary of the Treasury, Secretary of Labor, and Chief of Staff. It has many tribal wizards, Alan Greenspan for example. Its hunters are the Joint Chiefs, each with huge armies at their command. Its gatherers are armies of service providers in areas of health, welfare and housing, as well as the IRS who gathers tax revenues. Its Councils of Elders are the Senate and the Supreme Court.

Over the past 200 years, the hunting and gathering lands of the native Americans were invaded, conquered, and converted to cropland. Most of the original forests were cut down, the prairies plowed under. As the population of farmers and ranchers spread westward, protection from Indians was often provided by armies, and armies spearheaded the expansion to capture and control lands in Texas and New Mexico.

Farming communities arose with towns that provided supplies and goods as well as schools, local government, and the familiar white church building with a spire. In time, the land was divided — first into territories and then into states, each with its own Alpha, dominance hierarchy of state officials and councils of elders.

Not only does the US government encompass all the archetypal tribal roles, it also follows basic principles of tribal dynamics. All political governing bodies provide an arena, a kind of stomping ground where struggles for dominance and power are played out.

It does not seem to matter what political ideology is espoused. Communism, socialism, and democracy all eventually evolve into pyramid-shaped dominance hierarchies and those who are most intelligent, ruthless, and skillful in developing alliances rise to positions of great wealth and power.

No one has done a better job of describing the tribal dynamics of the US congress than the anthropologist Jack Weatherford. In his book, *Tribes on the Hill*, he draws an analogy by describing the arduous path men in New Guinea and Melanesia take to become political leaders known as Big Men.

> The young politician begins life, as do most of his peers, with a meager patrimony of a small garden plot and a wife to work it. The yam crop from this garden feeds not only the fledgling family but their pigs as well. If the young family works hard, they can produce an excess of yams, which can be used to raise more pigs. As they become prosperous, the young warrior acquires another wife, who can help grow even more yams and more pigs. The repetitive acquisition of wives, pigs, and yams lies at the heart of his political power. Through the distribution of pork to other less successful men, he acquires followers, and through his marriages to new wives and the carefully orchestrated marriages of his own children, he acquires allies.[42]

This pattern of hard work and the formation of allies parallels that of the Masai in Africa, except that the Masai acquire and trade cattle instead of pigs.

As Weatherford has pointed out, it also parallels the dynamics of politics and the acquisition of power in the US Congress.

> The political path of becoming a Big Man in the United States Congress resembles the route followed by...Big Men in New Guinea....The distribution of pork represents the heart of the organization in both cases, even if the Americans have substituted a metaphorical distribution of grants-in-aid and water projects for the living, squealing variety. The more pork he distributes, the more followers he attracts, and the more followers he attracts, the more pork he acquires to distribute.[43]

In Rochester, Minnesota, a few days before his tragic death, Senator Paul Wellstone participated in a debate with other candidates for his senate seat. He revealed that Norm Coleman, the Republican candidate, had received over two million dollars in campaign contributions from pharmaceutical companies, whereas he had received only $975.00. Of course, Senator Wellstone neglected to mention that he, as well as Coleman, had received tens of millions in total contributions. Big drug companies were only one source. Big insurance, oil, tobacco, agriculture, banking, health care, accounting, energy, communications and dozens of labor unions and professional organizations also stuffed cash into their pockets. Expensive advertisements for their campaigns began to show on television a full two years before the election.

By calling them "campaign contributions" rather than bribes, US politicians have convinced the voting public, and themselves, that there is nothing wrong with the massive tribute they extract from unions, corporations, wealthy individuals and lobbyists. There are no laws which require that these so-called "campaign contributions" be spent on campaigns, and in fact many of those offering tributes wait until after the election so that their bribes to gain influence will not be wasted. The staff of some lobbyists is larger than those of the congressmen and senators they try to influence and often these lobbyists arrive with a check in one hand and a draft of desired legislation in the other. Thus, big drug and oil corporations often write legislation that provides tax breaks and protection of their markets. Of course, every senator insists than the bribes do not

---

42. Weatherford, J. McIver, *Tribes on the Hill, The US Congress, Rituals and Realities* (Massachusetts: Bergin & Garvey Publishers, Inc., 1985).

43. Op. cit.

Chapter Fourteen: Nation-States as Tribes

influence them; but the massive library full of special tax breaks for various large companies and industries demonstrate that the money given to legislators pays big dividends.

The recent passing of a farm bill in the US demonstrated a simple, cynical formula. Huge corporations like ADM, ConAgra, American Crystal Sugar, and Cargill essentially said to Congress, "We will give you millions if you will give us billions." The poor family farmers who are always trotted out to gain the sympathy of the public received very little. They surely could not afford the massive bribes needed to garner the votes of legislators. The billions will go to the same huge corporations that are driving family farms out of business by controlling crop prices and markets.

Furthermore, when a congressman or senator leaves office, there are no laws requiring him or her to return the balance in their "war chests." Most voters are unaware that some congressmen and senators put large portions of these bribes into their personal bank accounts.

When naive and idealistic new senators come into office, they often rail against the massive flows of tributes and "gifts" from lobbyists. When the opportunity to become a multi-millionaire becomes clear to them and the checks start rolling in, their idealism wilts. It is not surprising that campaign finance rules have proven to be so resistant to reform. None of the recipients wants to kill the golden goose. Powerful party leaders who are in a position to distribute massive "donations" to the war chests of younger senators, and congressmen do not want to lose one of their main levers of power.

Perhaps the frequently used phrase "corporate greed" should be broadened to "corporate and political greed," particularly since those business executives recently convicted of fraud were major donors, passing out huge bribes to both parties. In earlier tribes, one of the main occupations of the potentate was to receive visitors, hear their grievances, and accept their tribute. Did these "tributes" influence the way the potentate responded to their grievance? Of course.

Using the "free speech" argument to justify these bribes is disgusting. If a person were stopped by a highway patrolman for speeding, would it be OK to offer him a $100 campaign contribution? Perhaps he would like to run for sheriff some day. Should this be allowed as an exercise in free speech?

POLITICAL DYNASTIES

In many nation-states, the transfer of wealth and power was and is hereditary. In Europe, China, and throughout Polynesia, including Hawaii, the alpha position passed from father or mother to son or daughter. Nepotism was the rule. Even though Big Men in many developed cultures no longer collect wives as a method of expanding their influence and power, marriages and the family relationships that result still provide important power levers. Although some of this has been suppressed in the US and other modern democratic countries which rely on elections, dozens of political dynasties still exist. In the election of 2000, both Bush and Gore were the products of family dynasties. Family names such as Kennedy, Rockefeller, Pell, Long, Byron, Fish, Byrd, Simpson, Dodd, Brown, Goldwater and Burdick have all accounted for more than one generation of office holders. Weatherford pointed out that "a quick overview of congressional kin in 1981 reveals fifteen sons of former members, three widows, two sets of brothers serving concurrently, two others who are brothers of former members, as well as assorted cousins, brothers-in-law, and nephews."[44]

As in all other tribes, the accumulation of power and wealth in the US government requires many years and those senators and congressmen who survive many elections literally become elders. The new crop of senators and congressmen that emerge from each election are relatively powerless. They wait humbly for committee assignments handed down by elders. They have too little clout to have much influence on legislation — certainly not enough to make good on the promises they made while campaigning. They must wait patiently, for many years, and win several elections before the senior members retire, die, get caught in a scandal, or lose an election. Eventually, if they are clever and ambitious, they rise to be chairman of an important committee such as Appropriations or Defense. They finally become powerful elders, able to command huge "contributions" and dole out committee assignments to the most recent freshman class.

With all its idealism and attempts to escape from some of the abuses of power of earlier nation-states, the United States seems to continually revert to the same kind of power struggles and tribal dynamics that exist in all human clusters.

---

44. Op. cit., page 137.

A similar process unfolded in the USSR, another nation that claimed to be founded on ideals of equality — set up as a classless society. In a short time it, too, reverted to old-fashioned power struggles and tribal dynamics.

Corporations and the Evolution of Nation-States

Just as the corporate culture is changing the agricultural institutions of war and religion, so also is it changing the nature and structure of nation-states. Nation-states used to be aggregations of counties and provinces, which were in turn aggregations of farms and estates. The armies of nation-states were assembled from farm workers led by landowners. Those who owned the largest estates and could provide the largest compliment of soldiers became power brokers willing to join forces with others, for a price.

Nation-states are evolving away from aggregations of agricultural estates into aggregations of corporations. More and more, the role of government is to regulate, control, tax, and protect the interests of its indigenous corporations.

In the mid-1980s, only a handful of truly multinational corporations with sales over one billion dollars existed. Now, mergers and acquisitions involving many billions of dollars are almost daily occurrences. Several hundred giant corporations have mastered the challenge of thinking and acting globally. These are the new *world tribes*. Some of them control assets that are larger than many nation-states. Phillip Morris has annual sales that exceed the gross national product of New Zealand, and Ford's economy is larger than the economies of Norway and Saudi Arabia.

When treads began to separate on Firestone tires, and Ford Explorers in the United States, Argentina, and Saudi Arabia began to roll over following blow outs, Ford's CEO appeared on television to reassure the world that the Explorer was still a sound vehicle. But there was something unsettling about Ford's CEO. He had a strange, hard to identify accent. He was surely not from Detroit. His swarthy complexion seemed almost Mediterranean. How could it be that a company as American as Ford could have a non American CEO?

Executives who rise through the ranks in the new *world tribes* can start out almost anywhere. They often work in several nation-states, serving as CEO in various operating companies, on their way to top-level positions. Their ability to grow sales and profits in a small operating unit gets them promoted to a larger one. They normally rise through larger and larger chunks of the organization, proving their capabilities with clearly measurable sales and profit results, before getting the top jobs. The process provides the global perspective needed to understand and lead a *world tribe*.

The typical citizen of the United States or a European country is largely unaware of how far the globalization of giant corporations has progressed. In their book *Global Dreams*, Barnet and Cavanagh point out:

> These worldwide webs of economic activity have already achieved a degree of integration never before achieved by any world empire or nation-state. The driving force behind each of them can be traced to the same few hundred corporate giants with headquarters in the United States, Japan, Germany, France, Switzerland, the Netherlands, and the United Kingdom. The combined assets of the top 300 firms now make up roughly a quarter of the productive assets in the world.[45]

Globalization is most advanced in areas such as financial services, communications including movies, television and the Internet; manufacturing with giant corporations moving huge factories like castles on a chess board all over the earth to take advantage of cheap labor and favorable tax treatment, and shopping at over forty thousand cookie cutter malls scattered throughout the globe, all with the same shoe, clothing, fast food, computer and perfume shops. Barnet and Cavanagh said it well.

> An extraordinary global machine has developed to make, sell, and service commodities and to render all manner of services, but no political ideology or economic theory has yet evolved to take account of the tectonic shift that has occurred. The modern nation-state, that extraordinary legacy of Madison, Napoleon, Bolivar, Lincoln, Bismarck, Roosevelt, Stalin, Mao, Nehru, Kenyatta, and the millions all over the world who have sacrificed and died for it, looks more and more like an institution of a bygone age.[46]

Conflicts over disputed borders have always been a factor in countries operating as agricultural nations. More recently, many of the nations in the world were defined by the European powers, who carved territories out of larger or differently configured alliances, and labeled them new nations, often in direct contradiction to those factors that contribute to the development of strong and

---

45. Barnet, Richard J. and Cavanagh, John *Global Dreams, Imperial Corporations and the New World Order* (New York: Simon & Schuster, 1994).

46. Op. cit.

viable "tribal" cohesion. Religious and racial bonds have been severed by these new borders, and incompatible neighbors have been thrown together. This keeps the receding colonial tribes strong, while preventing any new threat to develop from upstarts elsewhere in the world.

As the arenas for international competition shift from controlling patches of land to expanding and controlling markets, nation-states are becoming facilitators and partners with their indigenous corporate tribes. There is no doubt that the government of Japan actively assists its steel producing and automobile manufacturing corporations in capturing worldwide market share. The war in Iraq suggests that the immense military and financial resources of the United States, as well as its allies, can be mobilized to protect their access to the oil that fuels their industry. Farming subsidies in the US allow agricultural prices to be set so low that African countries cannot compete in products including food and cotton. These are all ways of dominating other tribes. The recent international embarrassment over the US government's steel subsides were just one example of the double speak approach when it comes to free markets.

As international competition evolves from territorial control to market control, standing armies are becoming vestigial organs. Their main purpose and mission of capturing and defending territory is gradually evaporating as other weapons evolve to take their place. Markets are still, for the most part, identified with territory, but the development of multinational/international corporations proves that the markets are cross-border. Nokia, for example, like Coca Cola, Nestles and Phillip Morris are impervious to territorial control. Sometimes, the US army intervenes outright — as in Iraq — when direct access to a crucial resource is in question.

ECONOMIC SANCTIONS

When industrialized nations band together and impose economic sanctions on a single nation-state, they are essentially banishing that nation-state from participation in the new world economic order. This new form of bloodless warfare has been tried on Cuba, Iraq, Libya, Chile and Yugoslavia. There is no doubt that such sanctions hurt the development of the victim nation-state. Without a US market for its sugar and restricted tourism, Cuba has become increasingly poor and run down, despite the immense efforts at developing their social and welfare institutions. Visitors from the US feel like they are in a time warp. Without active trading partners, their economy seems to be frozen in time.

Economies such as those in the USSR, China, and North Korea who attempted to isolate themselves from full participation in the new world economy were, in effect, creating their own economic barriers. Among their fears were the possibility that their fledgling industries would be eaten up by more developed international competitors, and that land and real estate would be bought up by dollar-rich foreigners before a realistic market pricing system developed. As long as citizens of these nation-states could not travel to the developed nations of Europe, Japan and the United States, they remained unaware of how far they were falling behind in standards of living. Their leaders, who did travel, obviously observed the growing wealth emerging in the industrialized world. They faced and continue to face enormous challenges in finding a way to join the global market without losing everything and being colonized or enslaved in a new way.

The bombing of Yugoslavia and Iraq, together with the economic sanctions, were particularly painful to citizens who had already tasted the conveniences and benefits of industrialization. As the worldwide economy advances, more nation-states become active participants, and millions of new people stop growing their own food and become corporate tribesmen and tribeswomen counting on good, steady paychecks, economic sanctions will become even more powerful weapons.

Military conquest is clearly more dramatic in the short run, and far more satisfying to generals; withholding participation in the big game and punishing nations by preventing them from participating the economy is less dramatic but just as onerous: it kills slowly, but just as surely.

The power and impact of economic sanctions will become far more effective than bombs in influencing and controlling rogue nation-states. Iraq's complaints about the sanctions imposed by the UN show that the impact is significant. Economic sanctions against Cuba have created a region of stagnation and economic decline. But few individual nation-states will be able to muster much impact on their own. To be most effective, many nation-states must band together, as they have done on several occasions at the United Nations.

There is another, perhaps more powerful form of economic sanctions, that requires no formal declaration or UN policy. Thomas L. Friedman refers to it as "the electronic herd."[47] They are the thousands of international investors who buy and sell trillions of dollars worth of stocks, bonds, and currencies daily. They seek safe havens for their money and provide massive capital infusions in nation-states that offer attractive investment opportunities. The electronic herd is skittish and can stampede if economic conditions become unstable. When this happens, the impact can be devastating. Capital flees, corporations go belly up, currencies lose their appeal, and entire nation-states sink into recessions.

The electronic herd is a cruel taskmaster. It imposes a degree of conformity to accounting and reporting standards that allow no hanky panky and severely punishes those who do not play by the rules. Thus, the electronic herd enforces adherence to generally accepted accounting and reporting principles which are steadily becoming a powerful new form of international mores promulgated by the corporate culture. Furthermore, the herd is not controlled by George Bush, Alan Greenspan, the World Bank or any other identifiable individuals or institutions. Those who are hurt by the herd have no one to blame.

The electronic herd is focused on the self interest of thousands of day traders and brokerage houses and clearly does not pay attention to what may be politically correct. Floyd Norris, a New York Times reporter who tracks foreign investment, pointed out that during the second quarter of 2003, while the US was waging its war with Iraq, and demonstrations against the Bush administration raged around the world, foreign citizens bought an unprecedented $129 billion of U.S. government and agency securities. Official accounts, mostly central banks, added $43 billion to that total. In all, foreign investors bought almost 80% of the net increase in Treasury and agency debt during the quarter and now own 38% of outstanding Treasury securities, more than double that of a decade ago.[48] Some would argue that it is even more troubling that, at the height of US security and military concerns, the US is increasing its financial insecurity, increasing its dependence on foreign investors to unprecedented levels. "Between December 1999 and June of 2003, world foreign currency reserves rose by $870 billion of which $665 billion was in Asia alone."[49]

---

47. Friedman, Thomas L. Op.cit. Page 13.
48. International Helarld Tribune, *Forigners Financed the U.S. War in Iraq*, Floyd Norris NYT Firday, September 12,2003.
49. Financial Times, *Funding America's Recovery is a very Dangerous Game*, Martin Wolf, September 28, 2003

NAFTA, the World Bank, the WTO, as well as the United Nations, NATO and the EU all recognize the global nature of the new world order. There is tremendous resistance to these multinational organizations, especially by those who fear the loss of their religious traditions, cultural integrity, and nation-state sovereignty.

MULTINATIONAL TEAMS

As multinational corporations grow and new ones form, the concept of nation-state boundaries, the territorial point of contention during earlier eras, tends to lose its power. The new world tribes own factories and office buildings in many nations. They employee citizens of many nations. They stimulate the economies and pay taxes to many nation-states. They promote and encourage international travel and communications.

Here is how one such organization integrated a cross-national team: a tunnel was to be built under the North Sea that would connect Denmark with Sweden. It would carry both trains and automobiles. An impressive collection of world class engineering talent and experience had been assembled from all over the globe. There were underwater construction engineers from the Netherlands, bridge builders from Sweden and France, and dock and waterfront developers from Denmark and the UK.

The project was highly political, not only for the governments of Denmark and Sweden, but for fishermen, ferry operators and ocean freight companies from other nations that used that part of the North Sea. The project was running into trouble. When dozens of inevitable difficulties arose, disagreements were going unresolved. Team members were running back to their firms for direction. Government representatives were demanding answers. Project leaders were having difficulty leading, and log jams were creating slippage in the highly complex schedule. As the pressure increased, nationalistic prejudices began to surface. The Swedes distrusted the Danes, the Dutch remained aloof, and no one liked the French.

The project was at risk unless the members of the team could be brought to drop (or at least, subordinate) their outside allegiances and develop loyalty to the new team that was being formed. The firms back home knew that their own interests would not be served as long as the members of the project team kept looking homeward; they encouraged their employees to create a new temporary tribe for this purpose. They had to forge a new relationship with each other, and each tribesman had to get comfortable with his own role in that tribe and learn to trust the others to fulfill their roles appropriately. They hired an outside consultant to provide a team building programs which involved a series of fun and challenging problem solving exercises. Once they got to know one another's personalities and talents, listened to each other solving problems, and experienced some shared adventures, and once they saw their leader meet some tough challenges head on, the tribe began to pull together. They began to trust their leaders and solve more problems on the spot. The project got back on schedule and proceeded more smoothly.

Corporations are learning how to inspire employees to commit not only to the company but to the project team, even knowing full well that the team is a temporary entity, and that in a few months or years, they will all go their separate ways.

Over the past decade, thousands of joint ventures and multinational project teams have formed to work on corporate projects. Differences in race, religion, and national origin that once formed impenetrable barriers must be surmounted in the name of corporate success.

CORPORATIONS AND NATION-STATE IDENTITY

When the first large multinational corporations took root and began to grow, their emerging power became a major concern to many nation-states. Multinational corporations were able to play one nation against another, hedge their positions to avoid fluctuations in currency, and transfer assets from one nation to another to avoid taxes. They could provide dramatic economic benefits by opening new plants in an area, and massive unemployment by closing plants. For a time it seemed that they had achieved a new kind of sovereignty and were no longer fully accountable to any nation-state.

In the early 1970s, Salvador Allende declared economic war on some of the multinational corporations operating in Chile. He abruptly nationalized their plants, aiming to minimize the interference of the multinational corporations over Chile's national interests; a risky move. He soon learned that the corporations already had enough power to combat him. Chile's national power disintegrated almost overnight. Its line of short-term credit shrank under the international banks' pressure from $220 million to $35 million in the first year of the Allende government. The parts, equipment, and supplies that plants needed from the US to keep Chile's industry operating were withheld or were sold only for cash. The price of copper, Chile's major export, was pushed down. The cost of Chile's imports rose dramatically.

On December 4, 1972, Allende spoke to the United Nations about his plight.

> We find ourselves opposed by forces that operate in the shadows, without a flag, with powerful weapons that are placed in a wide range of influential positions....We are faced by a direct confrontation between large transnational corporations and the states. The corporations are interfering in the fundamental political, economic and military decisions of the states. The corporations are global organizations that do not depend on any state and whose activities are not controlled by, nor are they accountable to any parliament or any other institution representative of the collective interest. In short, all the world political structure in being undermined. The dealers don't have a country.[50]

As Chile's economic conditions deteriorated, Allende's fears proved to be more than paranoid ravings. No armies opposed him. No bombs had fallen. Allende had increased his military spending from less than $1 million to over $12 million in the first two years of his administration, but his army had no one to fight. They stood at the ready in their spiffy new uniforms, with shiny new weapons, while the poverty increased about them and their country slid rapidly into bankruptcy.

Allende was correct in recognizing that multinational corporations were undermining the political structure of his nation-state. But his standing armies and military equipment were part of the old era, and he had no weapons with which to confront the new and powerful corporate culture.

Even though the new world tribes pay taxes to many nation-states and hire employees from many countries, all still have a clear nation-state identity. Ford is clearly a US corporation, even if its CEO has a foreign accent. Philips is a Dutch company, and proud of it. Toyota is a Japanese corporation and American workers in Toyota's US plants have no doubt that they are working for a foreign

---

50. *International Firms and Modern Imperialism*, Editor: Hugo Radice. Harmondsworth, Middlesex, England: Penguin Books Inc., 1975). Page 237.

corporation. So far, no world tribe, no matter how huge, has declared independence from its nation-state, enacted its own laws, hired its own army, or printed its own money. Some nation-states forbid foreigners to serve on the board of directors of their corporations, but other nations have no such restrictions.

In the US, where the issue of states' rights vs. the federal government is often debated, huge multinational corporations pay taxes to many states and submit to a variety of state laws. However, if the climate becomes too anti-corporate, or wages or state taxes become too high, they can and do close up shop and move to another state. Recognizing the economic kick a major corporation provides in jobs and taxes, states as well as nation-states actively compete to attract them, often giving huge tax advantages to make the move attractive. Like the wealthy barons of major league professional sports teams, large corporations with their sophisticated tax wizards can often play one state or community against another and apply pressures that feel like blackmail.

World tribes seek areas where operating costs are low and where local laws do not hamper them in any way. When US laws become restrictive, cigarette manufacturers shift their advertising focus countries that do not yet protect consumers against this type of health risk. Under-developed countries know that with low wages and lax pollution and labor regulations, they might be able to attract investment from industrialized countries — that is, they can get in on the ground floor of corporate development, by having corporations build their plants there.

Of course, when Ford and Philips spread their corporate assets throughout the world, they have a big stake in maintaining political stability. Countries who challenge their interests, or where wholesale class wars rage are far less attractive as locations for investment. Political unrest acts as a barrier to corporate well being. To participate in the wealth of the corporate tribal society, developing nation-states must provide a submissive, secure environment.

The political unrest in South Africa caused a significant slow down and interruption in the growth of its economy. Many major corporations pulled out. As conditions stabilized, the corporations are getting back to take hold of South Africa's natural resources.

When Quebec came under the control of French Canadians who passed new laws which made French the official language of the province, dozens of corporations moved out, to Toronto fearing a change in the controlling power. The result was a serious recession.

True, on a worldwide scale, the benefits dangled in exchange for unquestioned cooperation in world trade act as a powerful force against political instability including war. The new world tribes are leading this change.

Chapter Fifteen:
The Corporate Culture in China

Most futurists predict that the growth of the corporate culture in China will change the world.

China clearly has the potential for becoming the most powerful economic force on the earth, easily surpassing Europe and America.

In 1990, Nicholas D. Kristof traveled to a remote area of Gaoshan, a small hamlet in central China's Hubei province. He visited the Dai family, whose eldest child, Dai Manju, had just dropped out of school because the family could not afford the $13 in annual school fees.

Gaoshan had no electricity and was a two-hour hike from the nearest dirt road. The Dias shared their mud-brick house with their pig, and they owned nothing: no watch, no bicycle, no change of clothes...

> Since then, gaps between rich and poor have worsened in China, and so I decided to seek out the Dai family again. I thought I would find them still living amid desperate poverty and official indifference, allowing me to write a reality-check column about how the Chinese boom has boosted coastal areas but left the vast interior little changed.
>
> But then I came to the end of the old dirt road — and found it had been extended a few years ago so that now it is possible to drive all the way to Gaoshan. Every home in the village now had electricity. Two families even had telephones.
>
> As for the Dais, they are living in a six-room house made of concrete. The pig lives outside. The parents proudly showed me their stove, televi-

sion and electric fan. Dai Manju turned out to have graduated from high school and then from technical school in accounting, and such lofty academic credentials were no longer uncommon in Gaoshan. She and her two siblings are working in Guangdong Province, all earning $125 a month or more — what her father earned in a year.[51]

Kristof's anecdote shows how rapidly China's 1.3 billion people are rising out of poverty and embracing the industrialization through the migration from the farm to the city.

Older Chinese folks can tell you, "We used to wait for the newspaper every day to read about the latest thoughts and pronouncements of our leaders. Now, we go to our jobs and think about business, the sale of our products and the profits of our companies."

Foreign firms are busy building condominiums in Beijing — for expatriates working in China, initially, but just imagine what will happen when someone starts offering mortgages to the Chinese. Once credit cards and automobile loans become commonplace, the economic changes will be astonishing.

On October 15, 2003, China became the third nation in the world to put a man into space. China's progress in developing genetically engineered crops has already resulted in the wide spread planting of a cotton crop that resists weevils. These accomplishments are astonishing. They demonstrate that China's scientists have fully embraced the methods and theories of science that are prevalent in the industrialized world. The psychological impact on China's neighbors in Asia may be more important than the scientific achievement. When the U.S.S.R. put Sputnik into space, the psychological impact on the world, and especially the United States, was probably more profound than the scientific achievement. To the degree that Asians have felt inferior to Europe and the West since the days of colonialism, China's achievement establishes a new more proud and healthy self-image. And if subliminal racial enmities play a role in international politics, including trade relations, Asians may be more eager to embrace China's rapidly growing economy than to continue to contribute to the economic prosperity of the West.

Jane Perlez, writing for the New York Times, reported "The dominance of the United States in Asia, unrivaled for more than 50 years, is subtly but unmis-

---

51. Kristof, Nicholas D. *Will China Blind Side the West?* (The New York Times, OP-ED Tuesday, December 3, 2002).

Chapter Fifteen: The Corporate Culture in China

takably being chipped away as Asian countries look to China as the increasingly vital power, political and business leaders say.

China's churning economic engine, coupled with trade deals and friendly diplomacy, have transformed it from a country to be feared to a nation that beckons, these regional leaders say. This new, more benign view of China has emerged in the past year as President George W. Bush is increasingly being perceived in Asia as having pressed America's campaign on terror to the exclusion of almost everything else."[52]

Many Asian countries, including China, have little difficulty adopting the corporate culture. Often when a new manufacturing plant is built in a village, the village leader becomes boss and the entire village becomes employed. The tribal dominance hierarchy of the village transfers in tact to the new business venture, and the long period of start up time needed for the team to get acquainted and learn how to work together is avoided.

How will China emerge and how will its culture contribute to the further strengthening of corporate tribes? China has created the world's largest dam on the Yangtze river. Huge tracts of land are expected to be covered with green growing crops fed by the massive new irrigation systems. Devastating floods will be avoided and a huge new inland waterway that can transport goods safely will be created. New cities and towns are already emerging where old ones were inundated.

When China's millions of bicycle riding workers start buying cars, its traffic and mass transit challenges in major cities, already impossible, will have to be solved. All of the problems experienced in Europe and America that are the result of the emergence of corporate tribes will be multiplied in China.

The thousands of joint ventures in China exist because of the encouragement and permission of the Chinese government. Each one is a powerful seed. As they grow, they are changing China dramatically, just as they have changed, and are still changing, all the nation-states of the developed world. American corporations take the line that infusing the corporate culture into China will make them more like us, and will create conditions that favor cooperation. As these thousands of new corporate tribes grow, both China and its joint venture partners will benefit. Still, it will be astonishing, indeed, if it is not competition that will increase.

---

52. Perlez, Jane / NYT *Chinese are roding influence of the U.S.* Saturday, October 18, 2003.

Some US senators and congressmen seem bent on demonizing China, as though they need an enemy, a nation to hate. But those who criticize China for its harsh human rights need to be reminded that two million US citizens are in prison, 70% of them for victimless drug crimes. They were put there by senators and congressmen, many of whom smoke tobacco and drink liquor, and who are blind to their own hypocrisy.

Rivalry between China and America is not going to go away; it is being shifted to the national and multinational corporations. Competition is still at the heart of the corporate game, whether the tribes are local, national or multinational. But China seems to understand that friendly diplomacy and the building of cooperative trade agreements among Asian trading partners is wiser than the game of intimidation and militaristic posturing.

In his book *Can Asians Think*, Kishore Mahbubani, Singapore's ambassador to the United Nations, encourages the developed nations, especially the United States, to be cautious and patient in demanding that Third World nations adopt such Western values as democracy.

The Chinese Communist Party can no longer regain the tight totalitarian control it enjoyed in Mao Zedong's time. Deng Xiaoping's reforms have killed that possibility. Hence, if the West wants to bury forever Mao's totalitarian arrangements, it should support Deng's reforms to the hilt, even if he has to occasionally crack down to retain political control. The fundamental trend is clear. It is, therefore, not surprising that three and a half years after Tiananmen it is the "soft" and not the "hard" authoritarians who are in charge in Beijing....

In dealing with Asia, I am calling on the United States to take the long view. These are societies that have been around hundreds, if not thousands, of years. They cannot be changed over night...[53]

Nicholas Kristof recently observed that having a strong hand at the helm — far stronger than Americans are comfortable with — may be a crucial factor in bringing less developed countries forward through the wrenching changes they face.

---

53. Mahbubani, Kinshore, op. cit.

Chapter Fifteen: The Corporate Culture in China

The Rising Sun

Japan's miraculous emergence in the fifty years following the end of World War II demonstrated that the corporate culture can flourish in a country where there are bone deep differences in racial, ethnic, and religious roots. There is no doubt that "Western" concepts and methods were emulated, and that Japan's move from a feudal god king and what was essentially an agricultural society to a democratic form of government facilitated their remarkable transformation, but their own rich history and ancient culture also played a major role. Their culture already had taught them to relinquish their self interest in favor of the community's interest: they were already deeply committed to the tribe, first and foremost. When the "chief" set a new direction, off they went.

Japan's respect for authority made it possible for the leadership to mobilize the entire population to meet new goals. They educated millions of workers, managers and executives in the methods and technologies of corporate tribes remarkably quickly. Labor problems which still plague Europe and the US, and which sometimes serve as barriers to change, were less of a problem in Japan.

There is a lesson to be learned in the fact that modern quality control methods which recently swept through American corporations first flourished in Japan. Arthur Deming, the American who led the revolution in Japan, had a hard time convincing US corporations to try his methods. Perhaps due to tribal rivalry, the Americans resisted the idea that the Japanese were doing better. But when the quality of Japanese product, especially automobiles, put Detroit to shame and American manufacturers suffered dramatic losses of market share, they began to realize that Japan's more rigorous and scientific approach to measuring quality and eliminating glitches needed to be imported.

When Japan began to export new, improved ways of achieving quality, there should have been an earthquake. The flow of knowledge required to install the corporate culture had been flowing from west to east for over a hundred years. Now, millions of American and European workers, managers and executives were learning about and admiring Japanese methods and techniques. They worked.

In areas of business education, science, and civil administration, Japan now ranks at or near the top, and its work force is among the most productive in the world. Japan has accomplished this blending of Western and Eastern methods without sacrificing its rich cultural heritage. Mahbubani said it well:

It has modernized and is no longer a feudal society (several key ceremonies are conducted in tailcoats and Japan has one of the most Europeanized courts in the world), but the Japanese remain Japanese. While many Japanese teenagers look superficially like their European or American counterparts, their homes are Japanese, their souls are Japanese, and they are reverential towards their elders. And there is relatively little juvenile delinquency or crime. The deep glue that holds Asian societies and families together has not been eroded by modernization.[54]

Japan's rapid adoption of the new corporate culture and its rise to one of the most talented and capable industrialized nations on earth provided a powerful model for all developing countries, but especially for other Asian countries. It gave them confidence, after a long period of feeling inferior to those Europeans and Americans who colonized them, as well as a vision of what they might also accomplish.

THE PACIFIC IMPULSE

At various stages of development, millions of students and workers in South Korea, Taiwan, India, Malaysia, and China are rapidly mastering the knowledge and know how of the new corporate culture, including accounting, marketing, banking, corporate law, manufacturing, and human resources methods and mores. This common body of how-to knowledge, heavily laced with scientific methods, is being laid down over the top of Hinduism, Taoism, Christianity, Buddhism, and Islam; yet it does not seem to obviously refute or contradict these diverse religions, and corporate employees with wildly diverse ethnic, cultural, and religious backgrounds are working side by side without difficulty. Many of these nations are "corporate-ready" in the sense that they have always cultivated a sense of submitting to the hierarchy, and being willing to play the position to which one is assigned.

Ironically, the new tribal corporations, the Asian specifically, now set to function it in the context of the world at large, seem more comfortable with the requirements of the Corporate Culture than Americans, whose heavy history of individualism often leads them to resist conformity to team requirements.

---

54. Mahbubani, Kinshore, op. cit.

Chapter Fifteen: The Corporate Culture in China

As these Asian nation-states create their own corporate tribes and absorb the new corporate culture, the time required for catching up with the developed countries appears to be shrinking.

Furthermore, as these Asian countries create, explore, innovate and find new, better ways of managing corporations, their influence on the continuing development and emergence of the worldwide corporate culture will dramatically expand.

The benefits of developing a regional trading cluster in Southeast Asia and attempting to lower trade barriers among member countries were already obvious when the European Union was formed. Some Europeans and Americans worried about the emergence of new ethnic and racial enmities which might emanate from such a trading block, suggesting some ignorance of the immense diversity already within and among Southeast Asian countries. The active sponsorship and participation by Australia and New Zealand also demonstrate the diversity of key players.

The first steps of what Kishore Mahbubani has called the "Pacific Impulse"[55] have already surfaced in the creation of such organizations as the Association of Southeast Asian Nations (ASEAN), the Asian-Pacific Economic Cooperation Conference (APEC), and the Asian Regional Forum (ARF). Membership in these and similar organizations as well as attendance at their periodic conferences have continued to expand.

Since such meetings facilitate the formation of trade relationships, no one wants to be left out. Top corporate and government leaders who are serious about participating in this most potent of all emerging markets see these organizations as on the leading edge. Mahbubani pointed out that in 1993, trans-Pacific trade totaled $300 billion, 50% better than transatlantic trade and the gap was growing. As huge Asian populations continue to escape from agricultural poverty, and buy more television sets, computers, cars, home appliances, cell phones, and airplane tickets this new and massive injection of consumer demand will have a positive impact worldwide. Millions of Asians already have vastly improved standards of living.

A little over 120 years ago, Henry M. Stanley, like other arrogant adventurers from the men's clubs of Europe, trespassed over one African tribal territory after another on his egocentric missions. When he was unable to secure passage through tribal lands with bribes, he did it with bullets. When his party

---

55. Mahabubani, Kinshore op.cit

encountered warriors, he simply shot some of them. Not surprisingly, he was a strong advocate of the ban on exporting gunpowder to Africa. He and other colonizing nation-states recognized that guns gave them a clear advantage. Yesterday's guns are replaced today by the new corporate power. Could it be that other nations beyond the West will get stronger as their corporate tribes become stronger and more numerous?

The Corporate Culture in the Middle East

What would skyscrapers be without elevators? The corporate tribesman is the first to travel on smooth ribbons of asphalt in air conditioned automobiles while the music of great artists plays on the radio. No king sultan, pharaoh, or Pope of the agricultural era had ever experienced such luxury. No great leader of prior centuries had flown in an airplane or watched a movie. The amazing machines of modern men are a major element of his rapid advancement, but they cannot run without oil. And it was oil that so rapidly and dramatically launched several Middle East tribes into the modern world. In the past 30 years huge cash flows have poured into the Gulf states. They have amassed great fortunes, acquired the finest automobiles, homes, computers and television sets. Their shiny new cities are like heavenly oases with all the same elegant shops as Paris, London, and New York.

But they have only partially adopted the corporate culture. Their beautiful robes and head dresses demonstrate pride in their Bedouin culture as well as a deeply held resistance to conforming to outside influences. They have no interest in opening their books to outsiders or attempting to be transparent in their financial dealings. They have no need to attract outside investors or to look attractive to the electronic herd of international investors. Their great wealth and the power it generates has allowed them a degree of freedom to do things their own way. They still practice flogging, amputations and beheadings and adhere to the same strict religious rules and mores that were practiced during their nomadic past. Compared with corporations in other developed parts of the world, in Europe and the US, their organizations are more religious and less diverse. And they are still run by Princes and relatives of royal families.

Of course the oil is not evenly distributed and those areas without it are both dirt poor and still locked firmly in the religious thinking and values of the agricultural era. They have not yet traded camels for cars. For these Arabs, religion provides their primary tribal affiliation and they express deep concern that their wealthy brethren are being corrupted by such western influences as movies, television, rock music and the internet.

Arabian oil fields were initially discovered and developed by US and European corporations but unlike colonies in other parts of the world Arabian leaders were clever enough to eventually pry loose the grip of foreign corporation, one finger at a time. First they negotiated the right to determine how much oil would be produced. Then they took over decisions on setting crude oil prices. At that point it did not matter much who's corporate logo was above the door. Arab leaders had successfully gained control over their own oil resources. Of course, they had a clear advantage. The oil was on their land.

Oil has become a powerful bargaining chip, used by countries with large oil resources for political as well as economic purposes. In 1960, Iran, Iraq, Kuwait, Saudi Arabia and Venezuela met in Baghdad to form the Organization of the Petroleum Exporting Countries (OPEC). These five founding members were joined later by Qatar, Indonesia, Libya, United Arab Emirates, Algeria, and Nigeria. OPEC controlled enough of the worlds oil resources to exert tremendous pressure on developed economies such as the US, Japan, the Netherlands and Europe.

In 1973 , as part of a political strategy that accompanied the Yom Kipper War, Arab countries cut production and placed an embargo on shipments of oil to Western countries. Only two days into the war OPEC members, led by Iran and Saudi Arabia, demanded a 100% increase in the price of crude oil. President Nixon had been warned of the embargo if the US should increase military aid to Israel. But he went forward in spite of the warning and requested $2.2 billion to cover the cost of a huge airlift to Israel. Nixon's decision so angered King Faisal of Saudi Arabia they he instituted the famous embargo on oil shipment to the US. The result was dramatic; long lines of angry customers at gas stations and corporations such as airlines and trucking companies that quickly went into the red. The economies of the industrialized countries across the globe were severely damaged and by early 1974 most of the world was hit by the worst recession since the Great Depression of 1932-1940. The oil embargo was not suspended until March of 1974, after Israel agreed to withdraw from captured Syrian territory.

The embargo left Americans deeply concerned about their dependence on OPEC oil. This worry and the much higher prices for crude oil stimulated development activity in every area of the world where new sources might be discovered. Conservation measures were initiated and alternative sources of energy, especially coal and natural gas were expanded. All of these measures have gradually undermined the power of OPEC. Then too, when the flow of cash into the Gulf states slowed down, Arab leaders began to understand the importance of keeping their customers happy.

Competition and disunity within OPEC during the 1980's, including Iraq's occupation of Kuwait, have also blunted the effectiveness of the "oil weapon". Without full cooperation of its member states, OPEC's ability to extort financial benefits and political concessions in exchange for maintaining the flow of oil deteriorated. As member states increased their oil production in an effort to capture a larger share of the market, an oil glut developed and crude oil prices fell. None the less, Gulf states of the middle east still control enough of the world's oil resources to be able to threaten countries in Europe and the Americas where the corporate culture is most entrenched.

Texas oil men like Bush and Cheney fully understand the benefits of controlling Iraq oil's fields. They repeatedly denied that their invasion of Iraq had anything to do with oil. But the benefit to the US of controlling the price and production of Iraq's oil and of further undermining OPEC's control are obvious. The first objective of Enduring Freedom, even before the armies marched toward Baghdad was to send in commando units to secure Iraq's oil fields. When Dick Cheney's old oil company, Halliburton, was given the contract to help rebuild Iraq, without letting it out for competitive bids, only a fool could deny that securing and exploiting Iraq's oil was high on the Bush administration's agenda.

When Bush asked congress for an additional $87 billion to help rebuild Iraq, Dave Letterman told his TV audience "When you write your next check to the government, remember that Halliburton is spelled with two Ls." One of the primary reasons why the Bush administration refuses to allow the United Nations to take a more active role in Iraq may be that they have secured a new grip on Mideast oil, and this time they do not intend to let go.

The new wealth of Mideast oil barons catapulted the leaders of many Muslim tribes into active participation in the new corporate culture. World travel, the importation of consultants, technicians, and foreign workers, sending their bright young students to European and US business schools, and the eager consumption of all the luxuries the corporate culture has to offer; all of these elements are putting pressure on Arab traditions and especially their predominant Islamic religion. Exposure to so called infidels tends to reduce fear of them.

Living in countries where the corporate culture is most advanced, such as when Arab students attend school abroad, and when business leaders travel to attend meetings and conferences, tends to soften attitudes toward foreign customs and life styles. Once out of the Islamic kind of cultural straight jacket, it is difficult to put it back on. In other parts of the world, when workers join corporate tribes, compromises and accommodations have been made by the workers as well as the corporations that allow for, and sometimes encourage tolerance for diverse religious and political beliefs and practices. As this natural evolution occurs in places like Saudi Arabia, Kuwait, Iran and Iraq, those who attempt to hold fast to Islamic rules, such as the Islamic fundamentalists, fear that their control might be slipping away.

PART FOUR

CORPORATE CULTURE VS. THE AGRICULTURAL INSTITUTIONS OF ORGANIZED RELIGION AND WAR

Chapter Sixteen:
The Evolution of Religious Belief

Just as the knowledge of agriculture led to the emergence of new religions which spread rapidly and tended to blend with and replace the animistic beliefs of hunting and gathering tribes, so also is the emergence of science and the corporate culture leading relentlessly to an erosion of the power and influence of traditional organized religions.

When mankind discovered or invented agriculture, one of the more profound changes that occurred was an evolution in religious belief. Hunters and gatherers had animal gods. Trees, flowers, mountains, clouds, even rocks had spirits within them. Tribes created gods and religious beliefs from familiar surroundings. There are no bull, tiger, or shark gods in the religions of South American hunting and gathering tribes, but the jaguar is a major god. Monkey and elephant gods are big in India and Bali. The Plains Indians of North America worshiped the white buffalo. In Samoa, one of the major constellations is an octopus.

Concepts of the afterlife, like gods, were also created from familiar surroundings. In Polynesia, some tribal funerals involved putting the deceased person in a canoe festooned with flowers, then setting the body adrift in the ocean current. For them, the afterlife was somewhere over the western horizon. The Inuita expect to feast on reindeer meat after they die and the Creek believe they go where "game is plenty and goods very cheap, where corn grows all the rear round and the springs of pure water never dry up." The Comanches of the late 1800s looked forward to hunting buffalo which were "abundant and fat" after death; while the Patagonians hoped "to enjoy the happiness of being eternally drunk." Heaven for many tribes was much like life here on earth, except that resources were never scarce. The people of the New Hebrides believed that in the next life "the cocoa-nuts and the bread fruit are finer in quality, and so abundant in quantity as never to be exhausted." [56]

When humans discovered that the planting of seeds, including sperm, resulted in new life, the result was the rise of new religions based on the concept of fertility. Baal, of the Old Testament (the god that the children of Israel worshiped with their golden calf while Moses talked with the new God, on the mountain), was a fertility god. Rites and religious ceremonies, including the widespread practice of sacrificing or impregnating virgins, were geared to insuring a successful harvest. Some theologians believe that Christianity, with its emphasis on sex and carnal knowledge as sinful and celibacy as holy, emerged as an antithesis of the fertility religions with their fecundity ceremonies.

Looking at the evolution of religious belief in the broad perspective of evolutionary psychology and anthropology is difficult because our lives are short and our experience covers a very narrow time band. The ten thousand year era of the agricultural age has been a time where organized religions emerged and flourished. Clashes with more primitive hunting and gathering cultures occurred and the mythologies of hunters and gatherers were steadily eroded by the dogmas of organized religions. Perhaps it is more accurate to say they were inundated. Scratch the surface of the Catholic religion in Mexico and Central America, and up pop the signs and symbols of the native Aztec, Maya, and Inca belief systems. In many parts of the world, humble people pray to the gods of their organized religion as well as to older, more local gods. Their religions often blend the old with the new. The timing of many Christian holidays was chosen in order to subsume pre-existing celebrations of the winter solstice, the arrival of spring, and other ancient pagan traditions.

When Kilton Stewart[57] lived with the hunting and gathering Negritos of the Philippine islands, he described a world thickly populated with unseen spirits. An entire hunting excursion could be abruptly canceled by the warning call of a certain bird. Evil spirits could creep into a camp and take over the personality of a friend or relative. Storms, floods, sickness, and especially accidental

---

56. Spencer, Herbert *Principles of Sociology* I-I (New York: D. Appleton and Company, 1897.

57. Stewart, Kilton, *Pygmies and Dream Giants* (New York: Bantam, 1972).

deaths were blamed on invisible spirits. Everyone lived in a perpetual state of paranoia.

An afternoon looking at paintings in the Prado in Madrid or any other museum with early European art reveals that medieval minds were also chock-full of spirits. Cherubs, angels, imps, and evil creatures almost outnumber the people in the paintings created a few hundred years ago. There is little doubt that the belief in flying babies and demons with tails was widespread. It still is.

The popularity of modern TV shows such as *Touched by an Angel* and movies which depict spirit people, heavenly angels, witches, werewolves, vampires, and satanic demons suggest that even in the midst of modern science, ordinary citizens live in a world populated with mythological beings. The amazing popularity of Harry Potter with its trolls, ghosts, and unicorns as well as *The Lord of the Rings* with another cast of mythological characters demonstrates how eager both children and adults are to immerse themselves in magical fantasies. In our modern times, the apparent hunger to believe in aliens from outer space and UFO abductions is another manifestation.

The *Origin of Species* was published in 1897. The widespread acceptance of science and scientific methodology in corporations is less than 100 years old and it parallels the emergence of the corporate culture. The amazing progress in medicine, astronomy, chemistry, physics and all other fields of science notwithstanding, religious beliefs change slowly.

Religious notions of good and evil still have tremendous impact on legislation and on the daily lives of Americans. Legislators elected by voters with strongly-held religious beliefs try to create laws that force others to comply with their religious views. Right-wing Christians apply steady pressure to get their prayers into public schools and overlook the fact that some of the students are Jews, Muslims and agnostics. No doubt, they are sincere in wanting the nation to be run according to their interpretation of Bible scriptures, but their blindness to the beliefs of non-Christians represents a form of religious intolerance.

EVIL AND THE WAR ON DRUGS

This blindness is clearly a problem when it comes to the US war on drugs.

In the first six months of 2002, there were 19 homicides in the city of Minneapolis. Seventeen of them were young men killed in drug deals gone bad or in the deadly competition to see which gang would control the turf for selling drugs in certain neighborhoods. Compared with other cities, Minneapolis is relatively crime free. In Oakland, California, the homicide rate went over 100 in 2002, with the victims being mostly young black men. Los Angeles recorded 658 murders in 2002. In New York City, homicides in 2002 were just under 600 for the first time since 1963. All over the nation, and particularly in large cities, thousands of young men are killing each other every year. In the US, the leading cause of death among young men is homicide.

One of the main occupations among high school dropouts in major cities is selling drugs. No other job for which they qualify pays as well. The drug war currently being waged with US advisors and equipment in the jungles of South America is killing hundreds of young men, not to mention dozens of Colombian judges and politicians.

Fundamentally, the use of drugs represents a health problem and people who use drugs become less healthy. If they become addicted, or take too much, they may even die. They need treatment. As hundreds of ageing rock stars have demonstrated, drug addiction is often curable.

Yet, if we compare the number of people who die from over use of drugs, such as with heroine overdoses, with the staggering body count of those killed in the US war on drugs, it is plain to see that the war on drugs is killing far more people than it is saving. There is something illogical about saying, "Stop taking harmful drugs or I'll kill you."

Over two million Americans are in prison in the US, and 70% of them are there for drug crimes. The cost is staggering. It includes salaries of prison guards who must provide around the clock surveillance and supervision, the cost of building hundreds of new prisons, the cost of food, clothing, medical and dental treatment for inmates — as well as the cost of increased police and drug enforcement personnel and equipment. Add to this the cost of lawyers, judges, probation officers and social workers and the expense of running hundreds of thousands of offenders through a court system that is already glutted.

But there is another, less obvious but more pernicious cost: hundreds of thousands of families torn apart, children growing up without fathers, a burgeoning subculture angry at the government, the police and the country that destroyed their lives. Prisons are less frightening to young men and less effective in deterring criminal activity when so many are already familiar with the scene after going there to visit their fathers and brothers.

Chapter Sixteen: The Evolution of Religious Belief

Drug cartels amass fabulous fortunes in supplying enough product to satisfy the world's appetite for marijuana and cocaine; and it is ironic that the two groups most opposed to decriminalizing these drugs are the US congress and the drug cartels.

The subtle roots to the war on drugs have religious origins. Some religious legislators think certain drugs are *evil* and that using them is a sin. By demonizing drugs, they have blinded themselves and much of the public to the point where twenty-year mandatory sentences seem reasonable. Orrin Hatch, the senator from Utah who sponsored and pushed through such draconian legislation, is a deeply religious man. As a Mormon, he believes that drinking coffee, tea, and even Coca Cola is a sin.

But the war on drugs does not include alcohol or tobacco, two socially acceptable drugs that are both addictive and deadly. Those legislators who celebrated passage of the bill that required 20-year mandatory sentences for drug offenses by having a cigarette or a martini were obviously blind to their own hypocrisy. If US laws were truly logical, a relatively harmless drug such as marijuana would be as legal and accessible as cigarettes and those who sell and use tobacco and liquor would be punished with prison sentences.

Myths that Murder

It is common to apply the term *myth* to someone else's religion — never to our own. And when we learn of another cultures beliefs about God and the afterlife, we often find them quaint or amusing. Every religion has its stories about what happens to us after we die. Indeed, one of the primary functions of religions may be to help us deal with the fear of death. When someone we love dies, the notion that they live on in heaven, and that we will be with them again someday, is comforting. When someone is sick or close to death, belief in an afterlife sustains them and reduces their fears.

Some primitive tribes consider death a long sleep. A proverb among the Bushmen is "Death is only a sleep." In Tasmania, a man's spear is often placed in the tomb when a man dies so he can "fight with it while he sleeps." The corpse of a Damara, having been sewn up, sitting in an old ox-hide, is buried in a hole, and the spectators jump backwards and forwards over the grave to keep the deceased from rising out of it. The practice of talking to the deceased is widespread. The Fijians think that calling sometimes brings back the other-self at death. The Malagasy not only address themselves in an impassioned manner to the deceased, but on entering the burial place, inform the surrounding dead that a relative is come to join them, and bespeak a good reception.[58] Many tribes, in India, Bali, and Mexico leave food offerings for the dead, much as children in Europe and America leave cookies for Santa on Christmas night.

Ideas of heaven and hell evolve, and there are clearly thousands of such beliefs, as many as there are cultures. Christian notions of Saint Peter at the pearly gates, winged angels, and a paradise free of worries, war, sickness and fear are no more believable than thousands of other religious concepts. Milton's graphic descriptions of hell provided dramatic visual imagery whose influence is still with us. Fear of Satan, fire and brimstone following death may keep believers from doing bad things.

Mythologies probably begin with wizard storytellers who offered explanations of things like thunder, lightning and what happens to us after we die. They may sooth or frighten us, or simply capture our imaginations. Burl Ives probably had no idea that his rendition of "Rudolph the Red Nosed Reindeer" would gradually become wrapped into the Christmas mythology of Santa Claus, sleighs, and chimneys. It happened in our lifetime, but to a child, Rudolph has always been a part of Christmas.

Unfortunately, these "myths" are not benign. They can be powerful enough to propel massive killings, wars, ethnic cleansing, cannibalism and suicide bombings. Of course, they also inspire great art and music, and great deeds of kindness and charity.

When asked about hell, one elderly Jewish man said, "I know what hell is. I've been there. I was in the concentration camp at Dachau." The common expression "war is hell" may be close to the truth. Perhaps heaven is sitting around a table with one's spouse, children and grandchildren, everyone safe, healthy and happy. Perhaps it is hearing that the one you love also loves you. It may be what a mother feels when she sees her new baby for the first time. If heaven and hell are here on earth, then the demons of hell must be those who murder, torture, and create concentration camps and war. And the angels must be those who love, save lives, and make families safe, healthy and happy.

---

58. Spencer, Herbert *The Principles of Sociology Vol II* (New York: D. Appleton and Company, 1897) pages 155-158.

Chapter Sixteen: The Evolution of Religious Belief

CASTLES, CATHEDRALS, AND SKYSCRAPERS

We need not dig deep into the earth to find evidence of the major agricultural institutions. They still exist. Those which were most powerful displayed that power in their architecture. The largest and most impressive structures were created by the most wealthy and powerful institutions. In Europe, castles and cathedrals give clear evidence of the fabric and structure of power in the agricultural era. In other parts of the world, royal palaces along with shrines, mosques, and temples show the same basic pattern. In the Mayan architecture of Central America, the tallest and most imposing structures were temples. Small towns in Mexico are still dominated by cathedrals and white-spired churches that rise above the other roof tops.

If great architecture tends to be a monument to power, partially designed to inspire awe, to intimidate the masses, and to commemorate if not deify the men who built it, then the cathedrals of Europe and other religious structures clearly demonstrate the awesome power centers of the agricultural era.

Among hunters and gatherers, religion was thoroughly blended with all other tribal activities. Full-time priests and soldiers were part of the more complex stratification that arose from agriculture. Participation in religious activities and rituals became a weekend rather than a daily tribal activity, and the culture of organized religions with full time priests, took root and spread across the tillable land on all continents.

In every village and town that sprang up across the United States, a white building with a spire rises above the other structures. Every Sunday, farmers from miles around would put on their church clothes, put the family in the wagon, and swarm to church. They joined other tribesmen and women in religious worship. Except for the fact that many now drive to church in automobiles and SUVs, millions of humans all over the earth still regard their religion as their primary tribal affiliation. The major ceremonies that mark human life, weddings, funerals, and naming rituals, still occur in religious centers

However, in the last two or three generations, the power of organized religion is clearly weakening.

In cities all over the earth, the tallest and most imposing structures are now corporate skyscrapers, not cathedrals.

The FDA does not seek the advice and prayers of religious leaders in attempting to determine which drugs and medical devices really work. They rely on science.

Few corporate management groups seek out or pay for religious advice. There are no corporate priests. Corporate wizards are scientists rather than representatives of God.

Prayers and other religious ceremonies are increasingly rare in corporations.

The greatest advancements in knowledge have occurred in medicine, astronomy, chemistry, biology, anthropology, engineering, psychology, and agronomy: fields of science.

In contemporary life, with men walking on the moon, robots on Mars, videotapes of meteors striking Pluto, and a manned space station orbiting the earth, science inspires more awe than organized religions.

There is no conscious campaign to undermine religious affiliation by scientists or corporations. The vast majority of humans are still deeply steeped in their religions. But the living and thinking time of humans is more divided when they have multiple tribal affiliations, and the corporate tribe consumes far more time than others.

In earlier tribal forms, both hunter-gatherer and agricultural, all members had the same religion. In fact, common religious beliefs represented the core set of values that held the tribe together. During the agricultural era, most nation-states operated with an approved state religion and this pattern still endures, particularly in underdeveloped nation-states. In corporate tribes, employees of many religions work side by side and the informal taboo against discussing religions at work prevents both proselytizing and disruptive arguments.

CORPORATIONS AND THE RELIGION OF SCIENCE

It is important to note that many government agencies now served as the voice of science, insisting on an empirical processes that attempt to strip away emotion, testimonials, and persuasive presentations by inventors and corporate salesmen. Only scientifically proven facts, demonstrated in extensive clinical trials earn FDA approval.

The values and methods of science go far beyond universities and research departments in corporations. When MBO (Management-by-Objectives) concepts were introduced in the planning and goal-setting practices of corporations, they required the same rigor and stripping away of emotion and testimonials that characterized scientific research. All goals had to be measurable. Even staff departments which could not use budget dollars and sales figures to measure their contributions had to create target dates on their projects as a way to demonstrate their accomplishments. But some staff departments such as Human Resources, Accounting, Data Processing and Legal functions resisted being measured. When the Chief Council of a major railroad balked at setting measurable targets for his performance, the CEO applied some much needed pressure.

"How much did we pay out in passenger and employee claims last year?" the CEO of a major railroad asked. The Chief Counsel flipped open a folder and read off a huge number, several millions. "How do we compare to other railroads in that area?" Again, the Chief Counsel referred to his data and gave an impressive answer. They seemed to doing much better than their main competitors. The CEO turned to the MBO consultant and explained that the railroad had decided to hire some field representative who were good listeners — warm, kind, coaching types who would make fast face-to-face contact with passengers and employees who had made claims and convince them the railroad was truly concerned. Then they would try to settle the claim quickly. They wanted to see if this approach would be more effective and cost less than sending out attorneys who seemed to be polarizing incidents in anticipation of major lawsuits. To the tribal way of thinking, the railroad was putting gatherers on the front line rather than adversarial hunters. Judging from the data provided by the Chief Counsel, it seemed to be working.

After a few more questions, the CEO asked the Chief Council to forecast these same measures for the coming year, then review his forecast with the consultant. He said he wanted the results in one week. The Chief Counsel said, "yes, sir." After that meeting, the project went smoothly.

Results-oriented planning, management-by-objectives and many of the new programs to enhance quality are like establishing hypotheses in scientific experiments. They strip away excuses and provide objective criteria so that both the individual and his boss can agree in advance what represents good vs. poor performance.

Faith, prayer, emotional appeals, and testimonials do not impress or influence Wall Street analysts when it comes to evaluating publicly held corporations. Here too, the concrete reality of dollars, sales, profits, and earnings per share are all that matter. The planning and goal setting which precedes forecasts of corporate earnings are often created with the same scientific rigor that is required in university research projects.

The fundamental rules of the scientific method, so essential for making solid progress in understanding the world around us, were created and agreed upon by men and women with vastly different religious and ethnic affiliations. Jews, Catholics, Protestants, Hindus, Moslems, Buddhists, Agnostics, and Atheists work elbow to elbow in corporate research departments, all of them rigorously following scientific methods to create new products and solve problems that will advance human knowledge.

Intelligence Testing and Succession

Science has been creating another revolution, this time in the area of screening and selecting new employees, especially at leadership levels.

The widespread use of intelligence testing, beginning during the Second World War, has been driving a change in the evolution of human organizations. Those who rose to top leadership positions during the age of agriculture and prior to the advent of intelligence testing were the sons, and occasionally the daughters, of wealthy landowners. The intense preoccupation with titles and marriages into the right families helped to build political power and maintain the class structures of many societies. Those fortunate enough to be born into affluent families were accepted into the best schools, took jobs with the best firms, and eventually rose to leadership positions in their companies and communities. To some extent, being raised in such families was the best guarantee of preparedness and competence for leadership positions; now, education and preparation can be acquired through other means, and can be tested in more or less objective ways. This creates a new porosity in what was once a very tightly closed system.

Being the son or daughter of a wealthy alumnus who contributes generously to college endowment funds is no longer the only guarantee to entry into the preferred schools. Top colleges and universities now accept the most intelligent applicants, and they come from all over the world.

Herrnstein and Murray described the phenomenon in *The Bell Curve — Intelligence and Class Structure in American Life*.

A perusal of Harvard's Freshman Register for 1952 shows a class looking very much as Harvard freshman classes had always looked. Under the photographs of the well-scrubbed, mostly East Coast, overwhelmingly white and Christian young men were home addresses from places like Philadelphia's Main Line, the Upper East Side of New York, and Boston's Beacon Hill. A large proportion of the class came from a handful of America's most exclusive boarding schools; Phillips Exeter and Phillips Andover alone contributed almost 10 percent of the freshmen that year.

...An applicant's chances of being accepted were about two out of three, and close to 90 percent of their fathers had gone to Harvard....the mean SAT verbal score of the incoming freshmen class was only 583, well above the national mean but nothing to brag about.

...In the fall of 1960, the average verbal score had skyrocketed to 678 and the average math score was 695, an increase of almost a hundred points for each test. ...In eight years, Harvard had been transformed from a school primarily for the northeastern socioeconomic elite into a school populated by the brightest of the bright, drawn from all over the country.[59]

Reliance on intelligence test results for admittance to college has been a major factor in the United Kingdom, British Commonwealth countries, as well as much of Europe, Japan and America for at least thirty years, long enough to propel an entirely new class of individuals into leadership roles in corporations all over the earth.

Corporations also use intelligence tests extensively, to screen applicants for specific positions. But industrial psychologists who administer the tests have learned that although intelligence is important, it is not sufficient. Once on board, new and often more rigorous measures are more important. How the individual performs in meeting or in exceeding measurable sales, budget, production and profit goals takes precedence. Like tests, these measures are objective. Being the boss's son often does not help. Being white, a Protestant, a Republican, or from the right college or affluent family does not ensure success. Those who can dramatically increase sales, cut costs, or improve profits, no matter what their SAT scores may have been, tend to get promoted and percolate to the tops of their organizations. However, in many organizations, the "old boy network" still seems to over ride all of these scientific and objective measures, particularly at levels below the Vice Presidents.

---

59. Herrnstein and Murry op. cit.

At a time when most corporations are intensely focused on quality, rigorously applying all kinds of careful measures to their products, on time deliveries, customer satisfaction, and turn around time between orders and shipping; it is surprising that very few American firms measure the quality of their management. Even though most would readily acknowledge that the quality of their management is extremely important, and most believe that their leaders are particularly bright and capable, few corporations actually attempt to quantify it.

> Industrial psychologist have taken great pains to create management and executive norms, and they use them routinely to evaluate outside candidates. However, very few corporations could tell you the average IQ of their management or their top executive teams. There are valid ways to test and measure achievement drive and various leadership and inter-personal skills, but these important measures of leadership are also not much used to measure the quality of corporate management groups.

Corporate executives were willing to apply strict quality standards to almost everything else. The various organizations which give out prestigious quality awards have many pages of requirements covering almost all aspects of corporate operations, but none of them required scientific measures of management quality.

Major airlines are concerned about the quality of their management, particularly in the area of customer service. Still, as with many other corporations, promotions within airlines often rely primarily on the old boy network. When a Director is promoted to Vice President, he may build his staff of managers by selecting employees he had worked with in the past. Thus, if he had been in charge of a hub in St. Louis prior to moving to the corporate office, many of the new positions would be filled by former friends and colleagues from St. Louis.

At one airline, a program was launched to collect objective test data from 475 supervisors, managers, directors, and Vice Presidents throughout the customer service function of the airline. Each manager was also rated by superiors, peers, and subordinates on a series of management skills. The project included feedback sessions to everyone who took the tests as well as help in translating the results into individualized development plans. Thus, every manager knew his or her results, what they indicated in terms of strengths and weaknesses, and how to use the data to further develop their leadership and management skills.

Results of the study confirmed that the airline's customer service managers, as a group, were below average when compared with a management norm group. The average IQ of 117 was 9 points below the norm group average of 126. Measures of interpersonal and leadership skills, particularly important in the customer service function which included ticket counter, flight attendants, and gate and concourse managers, were also below average compared with the management norm group.

In a sense, these results were not surprising. Airline careers represent an alternative to college for many individuals. As a great many applicants who do not have college degrees are employed as flight attendants and ticket agents, the management group is likely to be less strong than in corporations where a college degree is an entry level requirement.

Results of the study were used to establish standards in areas of hiring and promotions, and this new policy created a mild firestorm. Managers who had previously had a relatively free hand in selecting friends and colleagues now had to pick those who would upgrade the overall quality of the management group. New hires also had to take the same battery of tests and meet or exceed the new standards.

Thus, there are trends and countervailing trends; but the net result that an increasing reliance on *merit* and on objective ways of measuring it have become a important elements of the corporate culture and it have begun to chip away at the class structures. In many Asian countries, as well as in Europe and the United States, this has had the effect of providing opportunities to young people who had no chance of being recognized even fifty years ago. The emergence of this new corporate meritocracy in places like China and India promises to release new levels of talent and ability that will prove to be formidable in the competition for world markets.

Although the corporate culture tolerates the many religions of the agricultural era and employs workers and managers who belong to vastly different religions, the concepts, methods, tools and practices of science have become integrated into the mores of the new corporate culture. Many of the older values remain. An employee caught stealing from a corporation may be fired on the spot, no questions asked. Lying and cheating is frowned upon. In many corporations, having sex with fellow employees is taboo. Physical fights are out of the question. But new rules pertaining to labor and employee relations, insider trading, financial reporting, occupational safety, intellectual property, copyrights, and patents have been added, and more are needed.

When Culture Clash

All cultures represent what Thomas L. Friedman called a "straight jacket." Each prescribes rules of behavior which include things its adherents should or must do, as well as things they must not do. Each culture also prescribes sets of rewards that will come to those who abide by the rules as well as sets of punishments for those who break them. These rules often shape every facet of life: what a person should or should not wear, what foods they should or should not eat, whom to marry, when and with whom to have sex, when and to whom to pay taxes, and what ceremonies, such as weddings, funerals, and rites of passage are required. A major responsibility of all alphas and elders is to interpret and enforce these rules. All cultures have judges who perform these tasks; these are typically older men and women who have developed wisdom and mature judgment. Rewards can range from promotions and advancement in the cultural hierarchy to great monuments, land grants, and financial rewards. Punishments can range from public disapproval and fines to prison, banishment and even executions.

When cultures with different beliefs, rules and requirements come into close contact, clashes great and small are likely to result. The past ten thousand years involved one war after another pitting culture against culture, with the victors invariably expanding their religions, languages, art and all other elements of their culture, while the losers' cultures tended to fade. The culture with superior technology and the most powerful armies was often able to convince people in less developed areas to adopt new ways of living and thinking about the world.

In the late 1800s the Mormons, in what was then the Utah territories, were still practicing polygamy and this was an intolerable annoyance to the larger and more powerful culture of the U.S. An army was sent to Utah to quell the Mormon uprising; officially giving up the practice of polygamy was made a condition of Utah becoming a state. Utah's representative in the Senate was a Mormon named Smoot who defended polygamy in the name of religious freedom, even though he said he did not practice it himself. One crusty old senator told his fellow politicians, "I would rather sit in the senate with a polygamist who doesn't polyg than a monogamist who doesn't monog."

When the Mormons were forced to give up polygamy, many families fled to remote areas of Mexico, Canada, and southern Utah. Families were torn apart when husbands renounced all but one wife. Even though polygamous groups still flourish, they are seen as outcasts by the main body of the Mormon Church and the differences between Mormonism and other protestant religions rarely result in such outstanding cultural conflicts.

Just as the Mormons were forced to give up polygamy, so also the tribesmen of New Guinea have been forced to give up the entrenched practice of head hunting, and in India the expectation that widows should join their dead husbands on the funeral pyres has largely ended.

When the Roman armies advanced north into Europe, they took their culture with them; and like many other armies they became unintended missionaries, scattering their beliefs, religions, art, foods, and DNA as they went. Christian missionaries from Europe and America were less subtle in blotting out native religions and gathering converts. This blending and mixing of cultures continues to this day. The paths of ancient migrations can be traced by identifying similar language patterns as well as by similar myths and tribal beliefs (as Claude Levi Strauss demonstrated among remote South American tribes in his book *From Honey to Ashes*).[60]

The Devastating Impact of Corporate Culture

The major organized religions of our time will not fade quickly. After all, the gods of the hunter gatherers in New Guinea and Brazil still exist and some native Hawaiians still believe in volcano gods.

But there are no more human sacrifices to volcano gods. In fact, there are very few pure Hawaiians. Where hunter-gatherers were overrun, first by agricultural tribes and more recently by corporate tribes, the blending of new cultures with old ones changes both. The impact of the corporate culture, with its amazing machines, its computers, TVs, cell phones, automobiles, and airplanes, and its scientific methods, can be devastating to human mindsets and belief systems.

The spread of the new corporate culture is occurring with stunning speed. In about two generations, the fundamental cultural values and practices of corporate tribes, including their reliance on science, have invaded every continent. Already the impact of the corporate culture is changing agricultural institutions

---

60. Levi-Strauss, Claude, *From Honey to Ashes* (Science of Mythology Ser.), 1980. Reprint of 1973 ed. Lib. Bdg. 30.00x (ISBN 0-374-94952-2). Octagon.

that date to the beginning of history. Large, extended families are becoming fragmented. Organized religions, though still powerful enough to shape people's thinking and world views, are no longer dominating many nation states. Science and technology are providing more credible explanations of the universe.

The diversity of corporate employees, especially in multinational corporations, results in greater tolerance of various ethnic and religious groups. A new, overarching type of tolerance is encouraged by corporations when people of many religions become employees and stockholders. The concept of Buddhists in China, Shintoists in Japan, Methodists in Tennessee, Catholics in Detroit and Italy, Lutherans in Minnesota, and Mormons in Utah all working diligently to help Northwest Airlines/KLM, or Coca Cola, grow and prosper is truly revolutionary.

The nomadic nature required of corporate employees, especially at management levels, also works to weaken competing tribal loyalties. When an employee accepts a job offer in another city or another country, he or she yields ties with family, friends, and groups and associations that supported and reinforced a sense of belonging.

Young anthropologists eager to study uncorrupted primitive tribes are out of luck. Every tribe, even the most remote, now has portable radios and children running around in Harvard T-shirts. The electric lights that sparkle all over the surface of the earth are new, by the standards of anthropological history.

RELIGIOUS FUNDAMENTALISTS VS. THE CORPORATE CULTURE

Modern corporations, particularly multi-national corporations, have no interest in attacking organized religions. They make no effort to convert employees to some different way of thinking or believing. They remain focused on their primary task — making money. But as the power and influence of the corporate culture spreads, many who hold firmly to their religions have become sworn enemies of corporate imperatives.

In her book *Terror in the Name of God*,[61] Jessica Stern shows that many religious fundamentalists, Christians and Jews as well as Hindus and Muslims,

---

61. Stern, Jessica *Terror in the Name of God* (HarperCollins Publishers, Inc. New York 2003)

believe that the corporate culture is corrupting the world. She traveled extensively to interview known terrorists and learn about their world views. In Arkansas, she met with Kerry Noble, second in command of a Christian fundamentalist cult know as the Covenant, the Sword and the Arm of the Lord (CSA). They believed that "humanists, communists, socialists and Zionists had taken over the U.S. government. They knew for a fact that Jews, Satan's direct descendents, were working closely with the Antichrist, whose forces included the United Nations, the IMF, the Council on Foreign Relations, the Illuminati, and the 'One Worlders.' They believed that major U.S. cities were like the Old Testament cities of Sodom and Gomorrah, ripe for destruction because of their wickedness. The cult had planned to poison residents of major cities. Believing that Armageddon was imminent, they had amassed a cache of weapons and began military training with the intention of bringing God's judgment down on those sinners who would not repent. In 1985, federal and state law-enforcement agents staged a raid on their 240-acre compound and after a three day standoff, the cult surrendered.

There are many similar groups in the U.S.: the KKK, the Aryan Brotherhood, Neo-Nazis and others who see the federal government and the corporate culture as corrupt. Most collect weapons, conduct military training, and preach a brand of fundamentalist Christianity that identifies Jews and Negroes as minions of Satan. Eric Rudolph, who set off bombs at the Atlanta Olympics and in abortion clinics, was influenced by these views as was Timothy McVeigh, who bombed the Murray Federal Building in Oklahoma.

After interviewing terrorists and extremist in Israel, Indonesia, the United States, Palestine, Pakistan, Kashmir and Indonesia, Jessica Stern described some common threads in the religious world views of those who sponsor or commit terrorist acts. Their enemies were sinful, corrupt, and evil. Their mission, for which they were chosen by God and would receive great rewards in heaven, was to cleanse the earth. Shoko Asahara, the leader of Aum Shinrikyo (who released poison gas in Tokyo's subway system), fit this pattern as did Ron and Dan Lafferty, the excommunicated Mormon polygamists who murdered a woman and her infant daughter after "receiving several visions from God." They too believed that the end of the world was near and that they had been chosen by God to help usher in the second coming of Christ.

The young suicide bombers recruited by Hamas to kill Israelis are fired up by religious zeal, as well as patriotic fervor. When Stern interviewed Brigadier General Nazir Ammar of the Palestinian General Security organization, he explained how these bombers are recruited. "They are young, often teenagers. He cannot find a job even though there is pressure on him to work. He has no money, no girlfriend, and no means to enjoy life in any way. He tries to find refuge in God, and begins going to the mosque frequently. Hamas members are there and notice him looking anxious, worried and depressed. They talk to him about the afterlife and tell him that paradise awaits him if he dies in the jihad. They explain to him that if he volunteers for a suicide bombing, his family will be held in the highest respect. He'll be remembered as a martyr, a hero. Hamas will give his family $5000, wheat flour, sugar, other staples, and clothing. The condition for this: he is not allowed to tell anyone." [62]

When Stern asked a young Muslim from Pakistan, a member of Mujahideen, if he was afraid of fighting in Kashmir, he said, "What is there to be afraid of? I pray for death every day. During my studies, reading the Koran, I decided to sacrifice my life for jihad. If I die in the jihad, I go to paradise. Allah will reward me. This is my dream."[63]

In *Warrior Politics*, Robert D. Kaplan states that: "Today's warriors often come from hundreds of millions of unemployed young males in the developing world, angered by the disparities that accompany globalization. Globalization is Darwinian. It means survival of the fittest — those groups and individuals that are disciplined, dynamic, and ingenious will float to the top, while cultures that do not compete well technologically will produce an inordinate number of warriors."[64]

The Hamas leader, Abu Shanab, in an interview with Jessica Stern, said "Globalization is just a new colonial system. It is America's attempt to dominate the rest of the world economically rather than militarily. It will worsen the gap between rich and poor. America is trying to spread its consumer culture. These values are not good for human beings."[65]

Sayyid Qutb, considered by many to be the father of modern Islam extremism, described Americans as "violent by nature" and "having little respect for human life". He described American churches as "not places of worship as much as entertainment centers and playgrounds for the sexes". He was particularly critical of Arab leaders, whom he described as arrogant, corrupt, West-

---

62. Opcit page 51.
63. Opcit page 123
64. Kaplan, Robert D. *Warrior Politics* (New York, Random House, 2002) Page 119.
65. Opcit.

ernized princes and autocrats. These beliefs are part of the standard curriculum in many mosques. Even though Saudi Arabia has recently begun to crack down on al-Qaeda extremists, they still funnel billions of dollars to fund various Wahhabi organizations, in Pakistan, Palestine, Bosnia, Kosovo, and Indonesia some of which are conducting bloody jihads.

In 2001, the world was presented with the spectacle of Islamic fundamentalists high jacking commercial airliners and flying them into the twin towers of the World Trade Center. This tragic episode is an iconic example of the conflict between organized religion and the new corporate culture. Islamic fundamentalists see clearly how Western influences of industrialization undermine their religious values as well as their social and political power. Blasting the gigantic stone carvings of Buddha with artillery and destroying the world trade center, which could be regarded as a temple of corporate culture, have a common denominator. They were justified by deeply held religious beliefs. Like the young Palestinians willing to die in suicide missions, those who carried out the 9/11 tragedies were deeply religious people.

Prior to 9/11, most Americans were unaware that militant Islamic extremists had declared war on them. Even after the embassy in Iran was over run and the ambassador's staff was taken hostage, they did not understand why the crowds of screaming Iranians were burning American flags and effigies of Jimmy Carter in the streets. Most Americans had never heard of Wahhabism, the militant form of Islamic fundamentalism that dictated war with the West as part of its doctrinal underpinnings. They were largely unaware of the rise in Islamic fundamentalism that had been sweeping throughout the Mideast and Asia Minor, pushing north into Bosnia, south into Egypt and Morocco and east into Afghanistan, Pakistan, Indonesia and the Philippines. Alexander Putin has tried to convince the West that the uprising in Chechnya was part of the larger Islamic expansion, which also shaped the war in Afghanistan. He is still calling for an international coalition to deal with the problem.

The dramatic expansion of the corporate culture is meeting significant resistance from many groups, especially religious fundamentalists who see globalization, consumerism, and the profit motive as threats to their deeply held religious beliefs. Where the corporate culture breeds tolerance of the religious beliefs of it employees, and mainstream members of various religious faiths who work in corporation can form effective multicultural teams, those who see their religion as their primary or only tribal affiliation are inclined to see the corporate culture as evil. Jessica Stern refers to "...terror in the name of God, (as) the gravest danger we face today".[66]

Of course, the expansion of the corporate culture, with all the benefits it can offer, must be balanced and kept in proportion. Family values, and other affiliations, need to be protected, too.

---

66. Op cit., page xxix.

Chapter Seventeen:
Corporations and the Evolution of War

Although hunting and gathering tribes often fought to protect precious hunting and fishing grounds, or to capture slaves or livestock, their combat could best be described as skirmishes or raids. In some cultures, such as in New Guinea, these tribal confrontations became a source of entertainment. The men would put on war paint, grab their spears and arrows and trade insults with enemy tribes across an open field. Sometimes a warrior would get hit by a spear; but if it began to rain, everyone would go home. Among the northern plains tribes of North America, competition between tribes involved a game called "counting coup". Creeping into an enemy camp and stealing a horse or a spear, or touching an enemy warrior while he slept was regarded as an act of great courage. The privilege of wearing and eagle feather was awarded to the young man who succeeded. The man with many feathers displayed his prowess as a warrior to others as did war chiefs who wore the familiar war bonnets festooned with eagle feathers. There were battles to control territory and they often involved bloodshed, but war as we know it, with large, organized standing armies made up of full-time soldiers, emerged with agriculture.

Throughout recorded history, which parallels the agricultural era, nation-state leaders seemed to see war as a natural part of their job description, their favorite spectator sport. Peace was no fun. The power game of intimidation and the expansion and control of territory was clearly one of their primary preoccupations.

Generals in every nation need war for fulfillment. Their purpose is directing war. Their dream of glory is to win a battle. The officer with combat experience get promoted faster. Some career military men yearn for war to boost their chances for advancement. For meaning, they need an enemy, a crisis. For public support, they need a fear of attack, suspicion of the intentions of foreign generals. Our modern warriors stimulate the terrorist paranoia just as they stimulated communist paranoia a few years ago.

Claiming that war is terrible and undesirable is politically correct. But until we are willing to admit that it is exciting and entertaining, that it provides adventure and glory, that it generates praise and honor as well as riches and prestige to the victors, little progress will be made to stop it. War is like bull fights: bloody, brutal, and entertaining. War is like the staged battles and gladiators fighting to the death in the coliseum of Rome; brutal, bloody, and entertaining.

Most if not all the bloody wars in the history of the agricultural era, the crusades, the inquisition, the conquests of the Mayan and Aztec armies, World War I and II as well as the more current conflicts in Northern Ireland, Israel, Kashmir, Bosnia and elsewhere: were justified by religious doctrine, the desire to promulgate one's beliefs and culture, to destroy an evil enemy and to expand one's culture into new territories. The ongoing battle over the control of Kashmir may well have killed over 100,000 Hindus and Muslims. Rape, torture, and the killing of innocent children is common. It is tragic that religious men who believe in tolerance, the Golden Rule and "love your enemies" so easily become holy killers for God.

The persistence and frequency of war suggests that it may have genetic roots, perhaps another manifestation of the animal drive for dominance and survival of the fittest. To rise to the top of a nation-state, a leader must possess unusual traits of competitiveness and a huge appetite for dominance. This passion for power does not go away when the election is won. It may tend to refocused on competition with other powerful nation-state leaders.

In the 200+ years since the United States became a nation, we have been at war with Great Britain, France, Mexico, Cuba, twice with Germany, Italy, Japan, North Korea, Vietnam, Nicaragua, Panama, Granada, twice with Haiti, Somalia, twice with Iraq, Bosnia, and Afghanistan. One of the most bloody conflicts was the Civil War, where the battle of Antietam took 23,000 lives over a period of

Chapter Seventeen: Corporations and the Evolution of War

about twelve hours. The fluid nature of our allegiances and hatreds would be embarrassing were it not for our short lives and selective memories.

But as we evolve into more civilized, better educated, more ethical creatures our hunger to fight and kill is diverted to more abstract forms of competition. Corporations are driving this change because they have found ways for human tribal clusters not only to survive, but to grow and prosper without shedding blood. We can expand and control our hunting (marketing) territories without bloody physical confrontations with competitors.

History may be demonstrating that war is too costly, especially with the advent of nuclear bombs and computer guided missiles. As multinational corporations and their nation states become increasingly enmeshed in buying and selling, tribesmen and tribeswomen in nation states all over the earth realize that healthy trading partners are essential to continued growth and development. The zero sum game is replaced with win-win game when corporations actively try to keep their trading partners profitable. The vision of thousands of vibrant and healthy multinational corporations, employing billions from many nation states, driving world wide prosperity, without bloody wars, is becoming increasingly desirable.

Japan's recovery and rise to affluence in the fifty years after the Second World War provided a powerful example of what could be accomplished when Western economic methods were embraced. With relatively little military spending and a sharp focus on economic development, Japan transformed itself into a world power almost over night. As Yergin and Stanislaw put it in *The Commanding Heights*, "No one could possibly think (in early 1950) that a Japanese automobile would one day be more desired, and a greater status symbol, than a car from Detroit."[67]

In South Korea, Taiwan, Singapore, and Malaysia similar "miracles" of economic growth have lifted millions of people out of poverty and in every case the men who guided these transformations wore the raiment of the corporate tribesman and employed the methods and technology of the new corporate culture.

It may be flower child idealism to believe that war is subsiding, that the emergence of the Corporate Culture is providing a more practical, humane and

---

67. Yergin and Stanislaw op. cit.

less bloody survival formula for human clusters. Zbigniew Brzezinski reminds us that the twentieth century was the most bloody in human history. It was,

> Mankind's most bloody and hateful century, a century of hallucinating politics and of monstrous killings. Cruelty was institutionalized to an unprecedented degree, lethality was organized on a mass production basis. The contrast between the scientific potential for good and the political evil that was actually unleashed is shocking. Never before in history was killing so globally pervasive, never before did it consume so many lives, never before was human annihilation pursued with such concentration of sustained effort on behalf of such arrogantly irrational goals.[68]

Although we have all observed recent wars in Bosnia, Iraq, and Rwanda, as well as bloody struggles in Kashmir and Gaza, we have also witnessed practically bloodless revolutions in the Philippines and Russia. We have seen the Berlin Wall come down, the peaceful reunification of Germany, and an end to the Cold War. The recent worldwide demonstrations against the war with Iraq were unprecedented in size.

> As multinational corporations and their nation-states become increasingly enmeshed in the complexities of international trade, the viability of bloody war decreases. Yet it is shocking how quickly and easily our lust for war can be aroused. Enlistments following the attack on the World Trade Center skyrocketed. Young men who espoused peace, who once would have moved to Canada to avoid being drafted into military service, suddenly became warriors eager to get revenge. Fear of the evil enemy creates mass paranoia. Leaders tell us the sky is falling and the military must be mobilized to prevent it. They remind us that our airports, water supply, food supply, ocean ports, railroads, nuclear plants, bus terminals, embassies, borders, schools, stadiums, chemical plants, cattle farms and pipelines are vulnerable to attack and need guarding. Multibillion dollar planes and warships begin to move like giant ants in a hive. To get public support and the required funding a sexy name like Desert Storm or Enduring Freedom is chosen as well as some elaborate sets and visual aids for briefing sessions and of course, some dramatic theme music.

---

68. Brzezinski, Zbigniew *Out of Control* (New York: Charles Scribner's Sons, 1993) Page 3.

Chapter Seventeen: Corporations and the Evolution of War

In his book *Martyrs' Day, Chronicle of a Small War*[69], the late Michael Kelly provided a ground level description of what was left of the retreating column of Iraqi soldiers on the road from Kuwait City to Basra as the first war with Iraq ended. He gives a chilling first hand account:

"A variety of bombs and missiles were used, but the chief weapon was the MK20 MOD cluster bomb. This bomb is a long pod of sheet steel that opens when it falls, to release 247 MK118 antitank fragmentation bombs, steel bomblets stuffed with high explosive. When these blow up just above the ground, they send clouds of heavy little razor shards whickering through the air at four thousand feet per second."

Kelly reported miles and miles of wrecked, charred vehicles, roasted bodies, the stolen loot from Kuwait City scattered among the bomb craters and fragments of shrapnel.

> The first body we came across was in a Toyota, half blown apart from machine gun bullets or shrapnel. The driver, swollen and wedged in place by the crush of his seat up against the wheel, sprawled out the door with his upper torso hanging upside down. ...Several hundred yards up the road we found a Dodge K car with another crowd gathered around. The car was as full of holes as a doily. Pieces and shreds of decaying flesh were stuck all over the dashboard. On the seat lay two fingers and half a third, all still connected by a webbing of skin...

The next day, on the other smaller road to Basra, Kelly saw another charred column of vehicles. He could tell the attack had come from the front of the long caravan.

> ...the travelers in the rear must have had sufficient warning, as they watched those in front perish, to leap and run away, so the dead tended to be in the vanguard. The first four we saw had tried to run and made it off the road and twenty or thirty feet into the sand when the shrapnel caught them and razored them full of killing holes.

Desert Storm and Operation Enduring Freedom provided ways for the industrialized nation-states like the US, with their advanced technologies of war, to demonstrate their awesome superiority.

---

69. Kelly, Michael, *Martyrs' Day, Chronicle of a Small War* (New York: Random House, 1993).

Wars such as Desert Storm and Enduring Freedom delight and entrance us. Reporters flocked to the war zones in such numbers that they occasionally outnumbered the soldiers. The embedded reporters during Enduring Freedom would never admit how much they enjoyed participating in the drama, danger and excitement of live war, but it was evident in their grainy picture-phone transmissions. TV ratings were so strong and sustained that regular programming lost much of its audience. The anticipation and build up to "the mother of all wars" was like a Mike Tyson fight or the Super Bowl, complete with trash talk.

When the battle started and reports began to come in, TV watchers around the world paid rapt attention to every urgent newscast. When it became apparent that there were massive casualties on the Iraq side, and relatively few among the coalition forces, American worries and misgivings of a few days earlier seemed foolish. A knockout in the first round.

In the sequel, the big Texas trash talk and patriotic references to liberty and freedom, immediately followed by brave poses, were laid on even more thickly.

> We secretly enjoy the saber rattling and patriotic posturing of our leaders, whether it be Churchill on the BBC, Hitler thrilling the Germans at his massive rallies, or George Bush proclaiming his simplistic philosophy of good against evil. As difficult and disturbing it is to accept, George Bush and Mohammed Atta had something in common. Both were thoroughly convinced that God was on their side and that the other was evil. And both were willing to kill thousands of innocent people to accomplish their goals.
>
> If we are ever to become truly civilized, we must let it go. War is no longer inevitable. We have let go of cannibalism. It is now just a shameful fact of our not too ancient history. We have almost let go of infanticide and slavery. Genocide deeply disturbs us and makes us send troops to stop it. War is a disease, a plague. Militant leaders, blinded by their distorted views of patriotism and appetites for power, are the infected carriers. The new corporate culture is the cure.

DOES THE EAGLE HUNT FOR FLIES?

The huge military of the United States and its $400 billion budget, massive numbers of uniformed soldiers, planes, ships, and weapons of mass destruction demonstrate how thoroughly America is locked into the old, concrete, territorial, zero sum thinking of the agricultural era. In his recent speech when accepting

Chapter Seventeen: Corporations and the Evolution of War

the Nobel Peace Prize, Jimmy Carter reminded us that the US military budget is greater than that of the next fifteen largest nation-states combined!

Many nation-states have dreamed of dominating the world. Hitler has been thoroughly castigated and demonized for his horrendous adventure that killed so many millions. The hidden agenda of the US military to dominate the world has become increasingly obvious as the number of military bases and soldiers stationed all over the earth has spread from Europe, Japan, Cuba, Turkey, the Philippines, and South Korea to Kuwait, Saudi Arabia, Bosnia, Afghanistan and Iraq. The US military establishment has another "don't ask, don't tell" policy that goes like this: "Don't ask why we still have thousands of troops stationed all over the world even after the threat of communism has subsided, and we won't tell." But most recently, the Bush administration hawks have finally come out of the closet. Vice President Dick Cheney and Defense Secretary Donald Rumsfeld have proposed policy changes and plans that will make the United States the undisputed ruler of the world ready to smash any nation-state that attempts to challenge it.

Colin Powell stated in front of the House Armed Services Committee, "I want to be the bully on the block" with so much power that we can "deter any challenger from ever dreaming of challenging us on the world stage."

The eagle's carnivorous nature and desire to hunt is emerging in the shift in policy from defense to attack using such spin phrases as "forward deterrence" and "anticipatory self-defense", and as long as Dick Cheney, Donald Rumsfeld, Colin Powell, and George Bush remain "stupefied by the romance of imperial power"[70] the United States and the world will be in grave danger, hated as all bullies are hated, the target of every terrorist who can hatch a murderous sneak attack. Bullies seldom pick on someone their own size. They seek smaller, weaker opponents than can be easily dominated. Iraq looked perfect.

Being mesmerized by the appetite for war prevents militant leaders from hearing those who appose it. Thus, when Iraq agreed to resume inspections for weapons of mass destruction, Rumsfeld immediately raised the bar. Now he demanded complete disarmament. When UN inspectors were unable to find any weapons of mass destruction (WMBs), Rumsfeld and Bush interpreted this as Hussein's diabolical cleverness in hiding them. The Bush administration wanted war, and those who opposed them were quickly accused of being unpatriotic.

---

70. Lapham, Lewis H. *The Road to Babylon — Searching for Targets in Iraq* (New York: Harper's Magazine — October 2002) Page 14.

Cheney, Rumsfeld, and Powell pushed and prodded, arrogantly ignoring the advice of other world leaders. Since Iraq's navy and air force were certainly no threat, and their army had already been severely reduced in the first war, the imaginary weapons of mass destruction (IWMDs) were essential to their justification of war. Cheney has stated that these weapons of mass destruction still represent the greatest threat to the US. If it worked in Iraq, perhaps the American people will swallow it again in Iran, Syria, or North Korea.

George Bush, Jr. may have killed more Iraqis than his father. Desert Storm casualties were estimated to be about ten thousand Iraqi soldiers. Early estimates of body count in Enduring Freedom were also about ten thousand. But in his glorious adventure to rid the world of the evil demons, the US army also killed two thousand civilians. More Americans were killed and wounded in Enduring Freedom than in Desert Storm. Saddam Hussein may have killed thousands of Iraqis during his 30-year reign, but the Bushes may well have killed more in a few months. And even after all the blood and tears, peace is nowhere in sight.

It would have been far less costly in lives, money, and world prestige to help rebuild Afghanistan and show the Arab world, as well as the rest of the world, that the US is more interested in keeping its promises and helping to pull thousands of good, innocent people out of poverty than in demonstrating the pin point accuracy of its wonderful new smart bombs.

The task of rebuilding Iraq and establishing a stable government provides another opportunity for the US to demonstrate its sincerity in keeping its promises. Helping Afghanistan and Iraq become active participants in the new worldwide economy may do more to ease tensions and defuse Arab hatred of the US than trying to it with aircraft carriers and smart bombs. The thousands of new jobs that would result from burgeoning corporations in countries where Islamic fundamentalism now flourishes would eventually soak up recruits for holy wars.

Defusing Jihad

The vast majority of mainstream Muslims do not approve of terrorist methods. But, like all other religions, they are interested in expanding their influence and membership and they may admire the fundamentalist ideals

Chapter Seventeen: Corporations and the Evolution of War

espoused by some of the radical clerics. The most effective method to ending the jihad against the West and its corporate culture has more to do with educating the next generation of Muslims than with military conquest. Indeed, sending armies into Arab lands obviously inflames their hatred, fulfills their prophesies of jihad and attracts thousands of Islamic fighters from surrounding Muslim countries to repel the infidel invaders.

Recently, Saudi Arabia has taken significant steps to deal with the root problem. Time Magazine reports that following the May 12 attacks by al-Qaeda on three housing complexes in Riyadh that killed 35 people, Saudi authorities in more than 100 operations have killed at lease 11 al-Qaeda suspects and arrested more than 200. In an effort to cool the rhetoric in Saudi mosques they claim to have arrested nine militant clerics and fired another 2,000.[71] The text books of school children have be edited to exclude references to evil infidels and include more tolerant messages from the Koran. At the same time, as the world becomes better informed about Wahhabism, evidence of Sadi funding of militant movements worldwide are coming to light. Many of the madrasahs, or Islamic schools, in Pakistan that produced Taliban extremists and affiliated Pakistani radicals are Saudi funded. So are some of the more strident Islamic schools in Indonesia called pesantren. Time reported that Muslims in Bosnia have received some $400 million since 1993, initially to help Bosnian Muslims fight the Serbs and then to rebuild the country and to missionize. Diplomats in East Africa say Saudi's influence in the region is minimal but growing, especially in Tanzania, where fundamentalists have taken over 30 of 487 mosques in the capital and have begun bombing bars and beating women who go out without being fully covered.[72]

Islamic jihads are clearly an international problem. They threaten many nation states. And even though many nations have taken an active role in attempting to identify and capture terrorists, the Bush administration's go-it-alone approach in Iraq has clearly alienated important allies. John Vinocur reports that "a potential trans-Atlantic breach has opened in the aftermath of the Iraq war that seems to leave Britain wavering between its exclusive, pro-American commitment to NATO and involvement in a European Union

---

71. *Time*, September 15, 2003, *The Saudis - Whose side are they on in the War on Terror*, page 40-47.
72. Op. cit. pages 47, 50.

defense initiative pushed by France and Germany." Some defense and security analysts see this as a "defining moment in U.S. European relations, a change in basic geopolitical orientations..." [73] With Powell spouting his "world bully" strategy and Bush pushing his "your either for us or against us" world view, it is hardly surprising that France and Germany might be concerned enough about U.S. ambitions to find an alternative to NATO. Even Tony Blair has apparently shifted his position from "no" to "yes" on whether his country would support the development of a defense capability within the European Union.

In his book *The End of the American Era: U.S. Foreign Policy and the Geopolitics of the Twenty-First Century*, Charles A. Kupchan identifies the unified Europe as the greatest single threat to U.S. preeminence in the world.

"Through a steady process of political and economic integration, the EU is erasing the fault lines among European nation states, holding out the prospect of banishing war from the continent."[74]

> Kupchan believes that "nations no longer have the same incentives for predatory conquest" and that a sustained period of peace in Europe will result in the emergence of a new economic power center that will undermine and eventually surpass the U.S. in its financial muscle. By contrast, the Bush administration, primarily made up of ex-cold warriors, seems to be stuck on the challenges of the past, squandering billions of dollars on military adventures while the U.S. economy slowly wilts. The battlefield has shifted. Someone moved the cheese. While the U.S. continues to invest in military dinosaurs, Japan, Europe, China and others are building the economic leverage needed for power in the future.

War is not inevitable; but the struggle for dominance clearly is. Powerful men will continue to play king-of-the-hill, scrambling for ascendancy, first within their nation states and then with other nation-state alphas. And the national leader who reaches the top will continue to become the target for other powerful leaders who would like to replace him or her. The world's alphas will continue to be admired and feared, given credit for successes and failures over which they truly had no influence. This tendency to deify and demonize alphas (on the global as well as the corporate stage) creates special

---

73. Vinocur, John, *News analysis: Britain's subtle shift on EU defense* (London: International Herald Tribune, October 14, 2003}.

74. Kupchan, Charles A. *The End of the American Era: U.S. Foreign Policy and the Geopolitics of the Twenty-First Century* (New York: Alfred A. Knopf, 2002)

challenges. Kupchan has shown that both "globalization" and "democratization" are seen by much of the developing world as "Americanization." Every initiative taken by world class alphas is regarded with deep suspicion, especially by competitors who wish to replace them.

Chapter Eighteen:
Spreading the Corporate Culture

Great leaders are those who can present a vision which captures the imagination of millions. Getting a man on the moon was such a vision. The idea was inspiring. Armies of scientists focused their talents and energies on the task and when Neil Armstrong took his "one small step" the entire world looked on in awe and amazement.

If the vision for America is world domination, it surely is not a very original one. It will not attract the enthusiastic support of the entire nation, nor will other nations support it.

America's leaders should create a vision to bring the Third World into full and active participation in the corporate culture within ten years. The armies that invade Afghanistan, for example, should be wearing suits and carrying brief cases, not M16s. Our marines, the ones who landed in Afghanistan and Iraq, should be our brightest, most focused and persuasive young executives and consultants. They should honor, respect, and embrace Afghanistan's and Iraq's unique cultures and lead them gently into the western model of corporate culture.

Imagine how America's stature in the UN would improve, and how satisfying it might be to persuade other developed nations to take part in such a program.

In this context, it is important to note that the economic growth spurt among so many Asian countries over the past ten to fifteen years, has been accompanied by an unprecedented period of peace in that region.

CLOSING REMARKS

Corporations are a favorite target of the young, of disgruntled employees, revolutionaries and some religious fundamentalists. Thousands of students and protesters of various persuasions all over the world criticize large companies for degrading the environment, for corrupting politicians with bribes, for being cruel and heartless in dealings with employees, for charging too much for their goods and services, and for being greedy with executive pay and stingy with employee pay. Many are repulsed by the idea of putting on a suit and tie every day or yielding their independence to some insensitive corporate supervisor. Many feel the profit motive is too selfish. They aspire to more ideal purposes and goals. Perhaps it is nature's way for the young and the poor to resent powerful leaders and accuse them of all that is wrong in the world.

What some of them do not comprehend is that earning a living almost always involves joining some kind of tribe. If they are successful in avoiding a corporation and become a teacher or a hospital employee, they must still learn to deal with the authority of the school or hospital administration. If they become a social worker they are joining a huge tribe, a county, state, or federal government organization, each with its own dominance hierarchy, rules and power struggles. If they become farmers or entrepreneurs they still do not escape. They must compete for customers, particularly for the big corporate ones. And they must treat these customers well and cater to their needs and desires. Unless they are independently wealthy and need not work, or are content to sleep in doorways and cardboard boxes they must accept the reality that Homo sapiens are gregarious beasts who live, work and survive in clusters.

There is no doubt that corporate executives can be greedy and heartless. History gives thousands of examples of how poorly workers have been treated, and how selfish corporate barons have been in using others to create massive wealth for themselves. Corporations still pollute our oceans with oil spills, clear cut virgin forests, slaughter too many whales and seals, cheat investors, and force employees to work in unhealthy situations that lead to disease and impaired health. No one should question the need for laws, regulations, and watchdog

Chapter Eighteen: Spreading the Corporate Culture

agencies to guard against the corporate greed and excesses that would otherwise flourish. In fact, every industrialized nation employs armies of lawyers, inspectors, and regulators whose entire reason for existence is to control the greed and excesses of corporate executives.

But there is little doubt that corporations and the corporate culture are improving the health, wealth and welfare of billions of humans all over the globe. In 1981, Richard Critchfield's book *Villages* provided first hand observations of village life in India, Indonesia, and Egypt spanning a period of twelve years. His descriptions of the impact of technology and scientific farming methods on the daily lives of millions of ordinary village people all over the earth are wonderfully encouraging.

> You might call it, yes, a great cultural revolution. But it's the real kind of revolution, when common sense tells enough people they've got to change their ways and they have the technological means to do it. Unexpectedly, and most desirably, as the villagers move into the last twenty years of this century, in most of them food production is rising and human fertility is falling. Contraception and scientific farming are producing, at last, a change in the general human condition.[75]

There *is* a trickle down, even to the most remote villages of the Third World. Since *Villages* was published in 1981, the pace of change has quickened through the use of new hybrid crops and technology improvements in irrigation. But e-mail, television, cell phones, and modern transportation are turning the trickle into a flood, a healing flood. These new technologies are allowing millions of humans greater independence from authoritarian governments who attempt to control the flow of information, better access to information and technological advances, and better educational opportunities than ever before.

The true revolutionaries, those who are sincere about world peace, eliminating poverty, promoting world health, eliminating torture, slavery, and the shedding of blood for political purposes, will embrace corporations, encourage them, protect them, join them, buy their stock and strive to make them better, healthier, happier more creative places.

Analyzing corporations from an anthropological and Darwinian perspective, as this book attempts to do, yields many conclusions and predictions

---

75. Critchfield, Richard, *Villages* (Garden City, N.Y., Anchor Press/Doubleday, 1981).

that other authors, experts in political science and international finance, have also asserted. We are living in an unprecedented age, an emerging paradise. None of us have ever experienced the worldwide protests that erupted as the US went to war in Iraq. No one had ever seen the peaceful meltdown of a nation as large as the USSR. Seeing the world as a giant struggle for controlling huge patches of territory is too simple, too grounded in the zero sum thinking of the agricultural age. As globalization advances, as world markets become increasingly integrated and our world continues to shrink, the advantages of creating and maintaining mutually beneficial trading partnerships are becoming increasingly obvious. The emergence of the EU and its cooperative trade agreements among member nations has provided a formal, peaceful forum where differences of view, competing interests and the struggle for advantage can be worked out without resort to violence. Emerging trade agreements and cooperative attitudes in South East Asia, and now China, are having a similar effect. Now, just as it did 100 years ago, peace has a good chance. Will we squander the opportunity again, in devastating world wars, or will the globalization of the economy enable us to see that cooperation is more in our best interest?

At various points in this book, the notion that humans may behave like colonizing insects such as ants and bees is presented, and this may apply to the way we seem to pursue war. One wonders how deep in our brain stems war may be implanted. The desire for war may be as ingrained in our behavior as the struggle for dominance in tribes. War may be endemic in the personalities of alphas who may be unable to control their desire to be king of the hill. For centuries war has been a kind of spectator sport where powerful leaders struggled for dominance. Most of them asserted that God was on their side, and lured their supporters with the notion of a sanctified cause.

All the great religions of the world promote some form of the golden rule; but it is easily rationalized away when one has been assured that the cause is righteous. Many sincere men who call themselves Christians ignore key teachings of Christ; they always have good reasons why they should not "love their enemies" or "turn the other cheek." It is a tragic irony that differences in religious beliefs have inspired the foot soldiers of most wars.

And yet, the continued rapid spread of the corporate culture may, at last, provide a new survival formula that will allow men and women everywhere to focus their energy and thinking time on new more cooperative and less violent challenges.

As science continues its accelerating accumulation of knowledge one can hardly image the world our children and grandchildren will inherit. Not only does stem cell research hold promise for curing many common diseases, some scientists predict that steaks and salmon filets will be grown in huge factory vats and that entire food industries such as ocean fishing and the raising of cattle, sheep, chickens and pigs will eventually become obsolete.

Some medical researchers believe that ageing is causes by viruses and that vaccines that extend life are a real possibility. The resulting surge in population, should such a vaccine become available, will present major challenges the world will have to face and resolve.

These and dozens of other earth shaking innovations may well be developed by the wizard scientists of modern corporations. We have entered a new era in the evolution of mankind. As a species, we Homo sapiens are becoming kinder, more humane, more healthy, more nurturing, less fearful of ghosts and spirits, better educated and less inclined to kill those with different religious beliefs, skin color and ethnic origins. The new tribal mutations we know as corporations are the fundamental building blocks of this amazing evolutionary transformation.

INDEX

A

accounts receivable, 23, 34, 50
acquisition, 39, 55, 60–61, 71, 92, 103, 109, 143–144
Actualized Corporate Tribe, 103
Adam Smith, 118
ADM, 145
Aerospatiale, 59–60
Afghanistan, 18, 189, 192, 197–198, 203
Africa, 18, 67–68, 84–85, 88, 144, 155, 164, 199
African Pygmies, 19
agricultural era, 10, 12, 15, 25, 56–57, 68–69, 76, 89, 95, 97–98, 128, 132, 164, 177–178, 183, 191–192, 196
Agriculture, 20
Agta, 19
Airbus A-320, 60
Al Ries, 53
Alan Greenspan, 142, 151
Alitalia, 59–60
Alpha, 77–80, 83–85, 87–88, 92, 142–143
Alpha and Vision, 85
Alpha role, 77–78, 88
America, 11, 84, 111, 115, 134, 137–138, 157, 159–160, 171, 174, 176, 181, 185, 188, 191, 196, 203

American Crystal Sugar, 145
Andy Pasztor, 61
Anima, 9–12, 17–18, 26, 28–30, 45, 49
Anima and Animus, 9–12
Anima as Bread Winner, 18
Animus, 10–12, 39–40, 44, 49
Animus archetype, 12, 40
Anthony Willoughby, 57
Anthropology, 5, 95
Antietam, 192
Arafuras, 91
archetypal role, 1, 30, 50, 69, 74–75, 101–102, 116
Argentina, 14, 147
Artemis, 12
Arthur, 70, 76, 118–120, 161
Arthur Anderson, 120
Arunta, 45
Asia, 18, 158–160, 163, 189
Asian Regional Forum (ARF), 163
Aspects of the Feminine, 11
astrology, 73
Attention Deficit Disorder, 134
Australia, 14, 18–19, 25, 77, 131, 163
Aztec, 69, 172, 192

B

Baal, 172
baby showers, 13
Bangkok, 131, 137
bankruptcy, 55, 133, 154
Barbarians at the Gate, 39
Barnet and Cavanagh, 148
Basra, 195
Beijing, 131, 158, 160
Bible, 10, 46, 79, 173
Big Men, 143-144, 146
Bill Gates, 76
Bill Russell, 84
Black Stone Rangers, 43
Blackfoot, 49, 99
Bloods, 43
blue collar workers, 10
board of directors, 1, 93, 112, 155
Bodos, 91
Boeing, 47, 59-60
Bosnia, 189, 192, 194, 197, 199
Boy Scouts, 43
Brazil, 2, 123, 185
British, 13, 79, 96, 108, 116, 181
Brooklyn, 115
Brown, 146
Bruce Willis, 41
brujos, 67
Buddhism, 162
Buenos Aires, 137
Buffalo Robes, 49
Burning the Bitches, 72
Bush, 146, 151, 159, 166, 196-197, 199-200
Business School Wizards, 117
Byrd, 146
Byron, 146

C

Cain and Able, 46
Cairo, 116
Camelot, 70
campaign contributions, 144
Can Asians Think, 117, 160
Canada, 15, 48, 184, 194
cannibalism, 40, 176, 196
capitalistic, 121
Caracas, 137
Career Counseling, 74
Cargill, 145
Caribs, 95
Carl Jung, 10
Carl von Clausewitz, 55
Carlson Companies, 4
castles of Europe, 76
Catholic, 69, 172
Central America, 91, 95, 172, 177
central Australia, 45
CEO, 64, 76-79, 85-88, 91-93, 98, 103, 109, 125-127, 131, 147, 154, 179
Chairman of the Board, 92
Charles A. Kupchan, 200
Charlie Ergen, 61
Chechnya, 189
Chicago, 131
Chief Archetype, 77
Chief Counsel, 179
Chile, 25, 117, 149, 153-154
chimpanzees, 40
China, 14, 57, 95, 116, 118, 121, 126, 146, 150, 157-160, 162, 183, 186, 200, 206
Chinese, 13, 55, 83, 107-109, 118, 157-160
Chinese Communist Party, 160
chivalry, 44
Christ, 187, 206

210

Index

Christian, 118, 172, 176, 181, 185, 187
Christian missionaries, 118, 185
Churchill on the BBC, 196
City Bank, 4
Clarence Darrow, 131
class systems, 83
Claude Levi Strauss, 185
Cleveland, 43, 112
Cleveland Browns, 43
Clint Eastwood, 41
closing the sale, 50, 52
Coca Cola, 58, 125, 149, 175, 186
cognitive elite, 135
cola wars, 58-59
Colin Powell, 197
collective unconscious, 9
Columbia, 10
Columbine High School, 44
Comanches, 91, 171
Communism, 131, 143
Compensation, 83
Comptroller of the Currency, 132
computer chips, 23
Con Agra, 4
Cook County jail, 131
corporate and political greed, 145
Corporate Archetypes, 7, 9
Corporate CEOs, 79
corporate culture, 4-5, 108-113, 115-118, 120, 122-124, 132-133, 136-138, 147, 151, 154, 157, 159, 161-164, 166, 171, 173, 183, 185-187, 189-190, 193, 196, 199, 203, 205-206
Corporate Gatherers, 33
Corporate Greed, 130
Corporate hunters, 47
Corporate Hunting, 47
Corporate Tribe, 101
Corporate War Dance, 52
Corporate Warfare, 55
Corporate wizards, 76, 178
Corporations and the Evolution of War, 191
Cortes, 88
council chambers, 1
council of elders, 1, 10, 92-93, 103
court priests, 9, 141
Cub Scouts, 43
Cuba, 149-150, 192, 197
customer service, 9, 23-24, 29-33, 56, 59, 133, 182-183
Czar of Russia, 25

D

Dai Manju, 157-158
Daniel Shore, 136
Darwin, 99
Dave Letterman, 116, 136, 166
Deal and Kennedy, 108
Deng Xiaoping, 160
Denmark, 152
Dennis Kozlowski, 131
Dens of Wizards, 70
Department of Labor, 132
deregulation, 121
Desert Storm, 43, 194-196, 198
Detroit, 147, 161, 186, 193
Dhimals, 91
Diana, 12
Dick Cheney, 166, 197
Direct TV, 61
Division Vice Presidents, 10
DNA, 40, 84, 185
Dodd, 146
Does the Eagle Hunt for Flies?, 196
domesticating the tribal herd., 24

dominance hierarchies, 36, 77, 79, 81, 83–84, 143
Donald Rumsfeld, 197
Downsizers, 129
Dr. Goh Keng Swee, 117
Drug cartels, 175
dueling fraternities, 39, 43

E
earth mothers, 28
Economic Sanctions, 149
Economics, 117
Eddie Murphy, 41
Egypt, 68, 85, 95, 189, 205
Eisenhower, 79
Elizabeth Wayland Barber., 2
Elvis Presley, 85
Enduring Freedom, 166, 194–196, 198
Engels, 96
England, 88, 154
Enron, 119–120, 133
Ernst and Ernst, 112
ethnic cleansing, 176
EU, 151, 200, 206
Europe, 3, 39, 43, 79, 95–96, 99, 111, 115–117, 120, 132, 137–138, 146, 150, 157–159, 161, 163–166, 176–177, 181, 183, 185, 197, 200
Evil and the War on Drugs, 173
Executive Instinct, 112

F
Father Role, 45
FDA, 132, 177–178
Federal Reserve, 123
female gods, 18
Female of the Species, 10
female pecking order, 35

fertility deities, 46
fetishers., 67
Firestone tires, 147
Fish, 3, 146
Ford, 147, 154–155
Fordham, 118
Foreign trade, 121
France, 25, 96, 116, 126, 148, 152, 192, 199
Frank Bruno, 11
Frazier and Gillen., 45
French Canadians, 155
Freud, 3, 39, 45–46
From Honey to Ashes, 185
Future Farmers of America, 43

G
Gathering as Shopping, 25
Gathering in Corporate Tribes, 23
General Motors, 4
genocide, 40
George Bush, 151, 196–198
George Gross, 86
Georgia, 86
Ghana, 117
glass ceiling, 9, 35
Global Dreams, 148
Globalization, 121–123, 148, 188
God Kings, 79
Goldwater, 146
Gore, 146
Great Britain, 71, 192
Guangdong Province, 158

H
Haiti, 192
Halloween, 69
harems in China, 85

Harlow, 28
Harrison Ford, 41
Harry Potter, 70, 173
Harvard, 117–118, 181, 186
Hawaii, 19, 118, 146
headhunters of Borneo, 43
headshrinker, 74–75
Hearst castle, 131
Henry Ford, 76
Henry M. Stanley, 163
Honeywell, 59–60
House Armed Services Committee, 197
Hughes Electronics, 61
hunters and gatherers, 1, 14, 34, 53, 68, 98–99, 101, 172, 177
hunting grounds, 2, 29, 49, 57

I

Identifying Alpha, 80
imaginary weapons of mass destruction (IWMDs), 198
India, 95, 117, 162, 171, 176, 183, 185, 205
Indian Givers, 99
Indians, 13, 19, 67, 71, 87, 99, 108, 111, 143, 171
Infanticide, 40
Intelligence Testing, 180
IOC, 123
IQ, 134–135, 182–183
Iran, 85, 165, 167, 189, 198
Iraq, 18, 43, 149–151, 165–167, 192, 194–199, 203, 206
Iron Curtain, 122
Iron John, 27
Iroquois., 91
IRS, 59, 142
Ishtar, 12
Isis, 12
Islam, 162, 188

Israel, 165, 172, 187, 192
Italy, 186, 192

J

Jack Trout, 53
Jack Weatherford, 99, 143
Japan, 13, 57, 107, 111, 148–151, 161–162, 165, 181, 186, 192–193, 197, 200
Japanese, 13, 107, 119, 154, 161–162, 193
Japanese culture, 107
Japanese teenagers, 162
Jason Hoffman, 44
Jay Leno, 116, 136
Jews, 13, 108, 173, 180, 186–187
Jim Brown, 43
Jimmy Carter, 189, 197
Job Hoppers, 129
Joel Kotkin, 13, 108, 112
John Lippman, 61
John Maynard Keynes, 118
John Wayne, 41
Joint Chiefs, 142
Joseph, 70, 121
Joseph Stanislaw, 121
Jung, 9, 11–14

K

Kali, 12
Karl Marx, 131
Katie Couric, 136
Kennedy, 85, 108, 110, 146
Kishore Mahbubani, 160, 163
Korea, 123
Kuwait City, 195
Kwame Nkrumah, 117

L

labor movement, 98, 132

Lancashire, 131
Landowners, 96
Lewis and Clark, 99
Libra, 73
Litton, 59–60
Long, 146
Los Angeles County, 43
Louis XVI, 25
Lufthansa, 59

M

Madonna, 116
Malaysia, 116, 162, 193
male bonding, 36, 48
Malinowski, 45
Management-by-Objectives), 178
Mandan Indians, 49
Manmoh Singh, 117
Mao Zedong, 160
Marines, 43
Marjorie Shostak, 19
market share, 14, 37, 53, 55–56, 58–59, 62–63, 102–104, 149, 161
Marketing as Scouting, 52
Marketing Warfare, 53
Martin and Voorhies, 10, 18
Marx, 96
Masai, 42, 110, 144
Mass mail campaigns, 62
matrilineal, 46
Mayan, 69, 177, 192
MBA and Executive MBA programs, 118
McDonald, 47, 58
McDonald Douglas, 47
medicine men., 67
medieval knights, 41
Melanesia, 143

Melville Island, 19
mentoring, 9, 27, 36
Merlin, 69–70, 76
Mesolithic, 2
Mexico, 67, 117, 137, 172, 176–177, 184, 192
Mexico City, 137
Michael Kelly, 195
Microsoft, 128
Mike Tyson, 11, 196
Milton Friedman, 118
Minneapolis, 173
Missiles and Bombs, 62
MIT, 117
Mohammed Atta, 196
Montezuma, 88
Mormon, 175, 184–185, 187
Moscow, 118
Moses, 70, 172
Mother of God, 12
Multinational Teams, 152
Multiple Tribal Affiliations, 12

N

NAFTA, 151
Nairobi, 116
native Americans, 67, 143
NATO, 151, 199
Negritos, 172
Neil Armstrong, 203
Neolithic, 2
Nepotism, 146
Netherlands, 126, 148, 152, 165
New Guinea, 45, 57, 68, 143–144, 185, 191
New Mexico, 143
New Zealand, 147, 163
News Corp, 61
Nicholas D. Kristof, 157

Nigel Nicholson, 112
Nixon, 123, 165
Nobel Peace Prize, 197
Norm Coleman, 144
North Korea, 150, 192, 198
North Sea., 152
Northeastern Luzon, 19
Northwest Airlines, 4, 186
Norway, 147
Nurturing in Corporations, 27
NYSE., 123

O

Office of the President, 84
On War, 56
Orrin Hatch, 175
OSHA, 132
Oxford, 117

P

Pacific Impulse, 162–163
Paleolithic, 2
pastoralism, 46
patrilineal, 46
Paul Simon, 137
peaceful reunification of Germany, 194
Peat Marwick, 83
Pedro Aspe, 117
Peg Neuhauser, 111
Pell, 146
Pepsi, 4, 58–59, 126
Peter Gay, 39
Philippine islands, 172
Philips, 4, 126, 154–155
Phillip Morris, 147, 149
Phillips Andover, 181
Phillips Exeter, 181

Political Dynasties, 146
Polynesia, 19, 146, 171
Pope, 69, 77, 124, 164
priests, 68–69, 76, 99, 177–178
Princeton University, 11, 117
prison population, 45
privatization, 121
Protecting the herd from predators, 32

Q

Quebec, 155

R

Reagan, 41, 123
rebuilding Iraq, 198
Riane Eisler, 28
Ricardo Lagos, 117
Richard Critchfields, 205
Rio de Janeiro, 117, 137
rite of passage, 14, 42, 70, 81
RJR Nabisco, 39
Robert Abrams, 61
Robert Bly, 27
Robert D. Kaplan, 188
Rockefeller, 146
Rome, 116, 192
ROTC, 43
Russia, 14, 96, 121, 123, 194

S

Saint Peter, 176
Salt Lake City, 123
Salt Lake City Olympics, 123
Salvador Allende, 153
Samoa, 118, 137, 171
Samurai, 61
San Blas islands, 87
Saudi Arabia, 111, 147, 165, 167, 189, 197, 199

Scopes trial, 131
SEC, 121, 132
SEC filings, 121
Senate, 143, 184
Senator Paul Wellstone, 144
shedding blood, 193
Shiva, 12
Simpson, 146
Singapore, 117, 126, 135, 160, 193
Skinheads, 43
Smith Barney, 71
Sophia, 12
South Africa, 14, 25, 155
South East Asia, 206
South Korea, 117, 162, 193, 197
Southern Airways, 86
sperm competition, 40
Spreading the Corporate Culture, 203
St Johns University, 117
Stanford, 117
Stanley Kripner, 72
Sting, 116
Stock ownership, 128
Succession, 180
suicide bombers, 187
Sun Tzus, 55
Super Bowl, 61-62, 196
Supreme Court, 92, 143
Sweden, 116, 152
Syngman Rhee, 117

T

Taiwan, 162, 193
Taliban, 199
Taoism, 162
Taurus, 73
Teenage Crime, 42

Territory, 57, 61
Texas, 115, 143, 166, 196
Thai baht, 123
The Art of War, 55-56
The Bell Curve Intelligence and Class Structure in American American, 135, 180
The Commanding Heights, 121, 193
The Corporate Culture, 124, 157, 164
The Corporate Tribe, 5
The Cultivation of Hatred, 39
The Devastating Impact of Corporate Culture, 185
the electronic herd, 150-151, 164
The End of the American Era, 200
The Evolution of Religious Belief, 171
The Lexus and the Olive Tree, 122
The Lord of the Rings, 173
The Origin of Species, 173
The Rise and Fall of the Third Reich, 10
The Rising Sun, 161
The Tribeless Remainder, 133
The Troops, 95
The USA as a Tribe, 142
The Wall Street Journal, 59, 61
Thomas L. Friedman, 122, 150, 184
Tiananmen, 160
Tinbergen, 80
Tiwi, 19
Todas, 91
Tokyo, 116, 119, 187
Tom Brokaw, 136
Toronto, 155
Totem and Taboo, 45-46
Touched by an Angel, 173
Toyota, 154, 195
Trade barriers, 121

tribal adaptations, 4, 12-13, 47, 68, 99, 124, 137
tribal analogies, 32
tribal chiefs, 5, 57
tribal customs, 15, 109, 113, 124, 138
Tribal Day Care, 20
tribal mutations, 2-3, 5, 142, 207
tribal territories, 57
tribal war rituals, 42
tribal warfare, 5, 11, 57, 65, 111-112
Tribal Warfare in Organizations, 111
tribal warfare rituals, 11
Tribal Wizards, 76
Tribes, 13, 67, 102, 111, 139, 141, 143-144, 171
Tribes on the Hill, 143-144
Trobriand Island tribes, 45
twin towers, 189
Tyco, 131

U

U. of Pennsylvania, 117
UFO abductions, 173
United Airlines, 98, 133
United Nations, 150-151, 154, 160, 166, 187
United States, 3, 13-14, 36, 45-46, 79, 92, 95, 98, 115, 123, 132, 135, 137, 142, 144, 146-150, 158, 160, 177, 183, 187, 192, 196-197
United States Congress, 144
University of Chicago, 117
US military budget, 197
USSR, 147, 150, 206

V

Velvet Carpet, 35
Versailles, 25, 131

Viagra, 71
Vice Lords, 43
Villages, 205
vision, 71, 79, 85-87, 130, 162, 193, 203

W

Walter Cronkite, 136
warrior archetype, 41-42, 44
Warrior Politics, 188
Warriors, 40-42
Weapons, 47, 63
weapons of mass destruction (WMBs), 197
Werner Von Braun, 71
William Clinton, 85
witch doctors, 67
Wizard Archetype, 67
wizards, 5, 9, 68-72, 76, 98, 101-103, 141-142, 155
Wizards in Mythology and Real Life, 70
World Trade Center, 189, 194
world tribes, 112, 147, 152, 154-155
World War I, 3, 18, 161, 192
Wyoming, 99

Y

Yangtze river, 159
Yergin and Stanislaw, 122, 193
Yugoslavia, 149-150

Z

zero sum game, 55, 193
Zulu, 73

Printed in the United States
16093LVS00003B/109-117